MY BIBLE STUDY BOOK (SENIORS)

VOLUME 1

MINI THOMAS | BERLIN CHANDRA | NISSY VARGHESE | MONISHA STEEVE

Dedicated to all the Partners of Master's Grace Church Family.

Contents

Contents

Italics, Bold, underline in Scripture quotations reflect the author's added emphasis. Details in some anecdotes and stories have been changed to protect the identities of the persons involved.

Preface

"Jesus said, "Let the little children come to Me, and do not hinder them, for the Kingdom of Heaven belongs to such as these." (Matthew 19:14)"

Blanco

This verse from the Gospel according to Matthew, shows the heart of our Lord Jesus towards children. Jesus taught people of all walks of life- old, young, male, female; and children were no exception. In fact, Jesus loves children. At Master's Grace Church, we recognize the importance of training a child in the ways of God.

This book is the first of a three-volume curriculum, developed to teach the Bible and train children in a systematic and practical way. The plan is to cover the entire Bible in 3 years. Though there are many resources available, we developed this book to help children study the Bible, understand the Scriptures and learn how they can be practically applied to their daily life. We have used the READ approach to make this book be a very effective tool to the learner. You will notice that this approach is consistent across all the chapters and in every level and volume. READ stands for:

R- Read (reading the Scripture Portion from the Bible)
E- Explain (explaining the portion)
A- Apprehend (understanding it in a practical context)
D- Do (activity or application in everyday life)

Every lesson is integrated with a Memory verse. We have also added a Christ Connect section in every chapter. This is added to help the children see and understand how Jesus Christ is connected to our life through those stories. We also want to connect each story or Scripture with the great plan of God's salvation that is available through Jesus Christ. This book is for Juniors between the ages of 10 to 13 years. We have made this book available to suit the need of children across other age groups as well:

Kindergarten- Age 2 to 5,
Juniors- Age 6 to 9, and
Teens- Age 14 to 17

We pray that this book will be a blessing to many children in Jesus' Name. Amen.

Acknowledgements

Thank and Praise God for His grace and mercy. May He be pleased to use this work for His glory and the glory of His Church.

Thanking every member of the Master's Grace Church for their continual support, prayer and encouragement throughout.

Thank you, Pastor Joseph Thomas, for the drive, motivation and continuous guidance all through the process and for making sure this book happened.

Sincere thanks to our family and everyone who supported directly or indirectly! Special thanks to Mathew Thomas and Divya H. Kannan.

Prologue

Packed with application-oriented activities, the My Bible Study Book is a guide to help children develop and strengthen their spiritual appetite through reading and studying the Bible. This book is written for little children to grow in the knowledge of God. Teachers, leaders, pastors and parents would find this book helpful to teach the Bible to little children in a systematic and engaging way. As you embark upon this exciting journey, remember to:

Enjoy your journey!

CHAPTER ONE

BIBLE OVERVIEW

Session Starter

Let children to turn to the table of contents in their Bibles and ask, “How many books are in the Bible? Say, we are going to start reading and learning the bible in order so let’s start with a video on the books of the bible in order https://www.youtube.com/watch?v=LuyEryHeB6U

Psalm 119:105, 2 Timothy 3:16-17

Explain

"All Scripture is God-breathed and is useful for teaching, rebuking, correcting and training in righteousness, so that the servant of God may be thoroughly equipped for every good work." (2 Timothy 3:16-17) As we read, everything in the Bible is God-breathed, and the Holy Spirit led each author. Say, "Everything in the Bible can be trusted as truth because God continues to speak the same message of salvation and redemption in every book!"

Today, we will study how the books of the Bible were chosen and organized.

Many people look at the Bible as one book written by one author; this is not the case with the Bible. What makes the Bible unique is that it is one book; however, it was written by about 40 different authors and spanned over 1600 years (1500 BC to 95 AD). In essence, the Bible is a compilation of different books written under the inspiration of the Holy Spirit. What is more unique is that many of the authors did not even know each other, meet each other, or discuss with each other, yet there is a continuous flow in the theme throughout the book. Only the hand of God could cause something to happen to that degree with that many different authors and that great a time span between the first book written and the last.

The books of the Old Testament were written somewhere between 1500 BC and 400 BC. One of the things to recognize is there is a gap between the last book written in the Old Testament and the beginning of the New Testament. This gap lasts about 400 years.

The books of the New Testament were written somewhere between 45-90 AD. However, the Canon of the New Testament was not finalized until about 397 AD.

Now that we have an idea of how the period Bible was written, we will now briefly see how the different books were chosen to be included in the Bible. The different books chosen to be included in the Bible passed through the Canon of scripture. The term canon, from a Hebrew-Greek word meaning "cane" or "measuring rod," meaning "norm" or "rule of faith," was used to form the "collection of books" in the old and New Testaments. These books were tested to form the original and authoritative written rule of the faith and practice of the Christian Church.

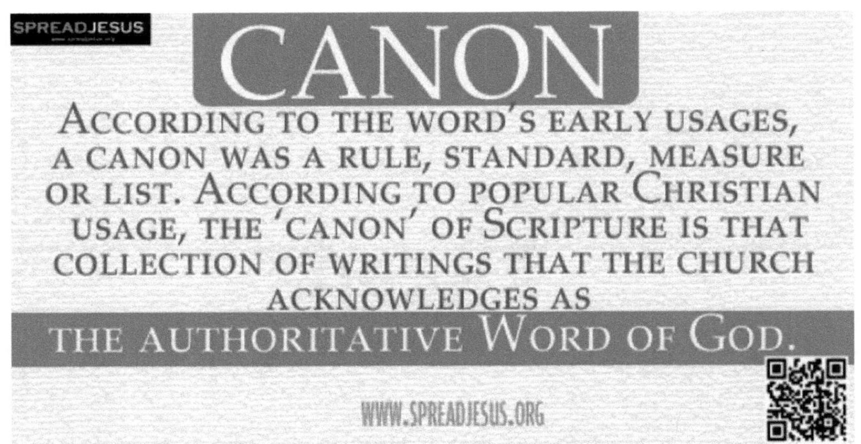

The Bible provides us with a Godly standard and measure to live on this earth and live a Christ-centered life and bring heaven on earth as we live in this world.

Let us now understand the layout of the Bible. There are total of 66 books in the Bible; 39 books in the old testament and 27 books in the new testament (teachers will briefly explain as per the age group the different categories of the books of the Bible in the old and new testament).

The different types of books in the old testament are:

- The Books of Moses or Pentateuch (Genesis to Deuteronomy)
- Historical Books (Joshua to Esther)
- Wisdom and Poetry (Job to Song of Solomon)
- Major Prophets (Isaiah to Daniel)
- Minor Prophets (Hosea to Malachi)

The Books of Moses or Pentateuch (Genesis to Deuteronomy): "In these books, God established the Jewish nation as his chosen people – the people from whom the Messiah would one day come!"

Historical Books (Joshua to Esther): Joshua to Esther are historical books that show God as the protector of those who believes in him and that he is true to his word by punishing evil and rewarding those who believe in his plan.

Wisdom and Poetry (Job to Song of Solomon): The books from Job to Song of Solomon consist of wise sayings, metaphors, psalms (songs), and poetry. These types of writings show the majesty of God and the power of his spirit in different ways.

Major Prophets (Isaiah to Daniel): The prophets speak of times to come of God's judgment, redemption, and overall future destruction of sin.

Minor Prophets (Hosea to Malachi): These books are "minor" prophetic books because of their shorter length (than the major prophetic books). They were also written for the same reasons as the major prophetic books.

And there was a time period of about 400 years between the Old Testament and New Testament.

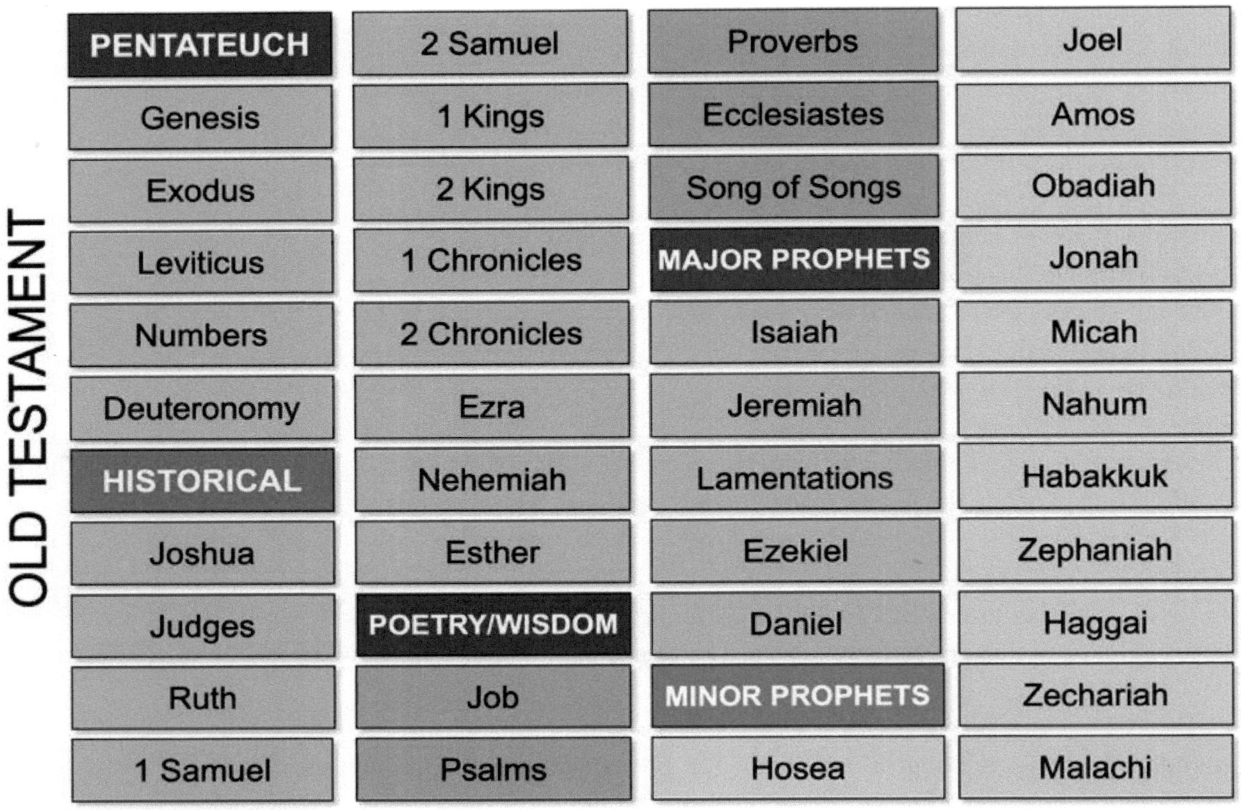

OLD TESTAMENT

PENTATEUCH	2 Samuel	Proverbs	Joel
Genesis	1 Kings	Ecclesiastes	Amos
Exodus	2 Kings	Song of Songs	Obadiah
Leviticus	1 Chronicles	MAJOR PROPHETS	Jonah
Numbers	2 Chronicles	Isaiah	Micah
Deuteronomy	Ezra	Jeremiah	Nahum
HISTORICAL	Nehemiah	Lamentations	Habakkuk
Joshua	Esther	Ezekiel	Zephaniah
Judges	POETRY/WISDOM	Daniel	Haggai
Ruth	Job	MINOR PROPHETS	Zechariah
1 Samuel	Psalms	Hosea	Malachi

Source: Bible Layout

The different types of books in the new testament are:

- Historical Books (Matthew to John)
- Acts (Acts of the Apostles)
- Paul's Letters (Romans to Philemon)
- Additional Letters (Hebrews-Jude)
- Revelation (apocalyptic book)

Historical Books (Matthew to John): These books tell us about Jesus' life, death, and resurrection.

Acts: This book tells us about the establishment of the New Testament church.

Paul's Letters (Romans to Philemon): These letters remind us how to live and act as believers in Jesus.

Additional Letters (Hebrews-Jude): Paul was not the only one who wrote letters – the rest of the books in the New Testament were also letters written by people such as Peter, John, and James, the brother of Jesus. These letters also remind us how to live and act as Christians.

Revelation: is the apocalyptic prophecy (which tells about the things to come). The book's purpose was to strengthen the faith of the members of these churches by assuring them that deliverance from the evil powers arrayed against them was close at hand.

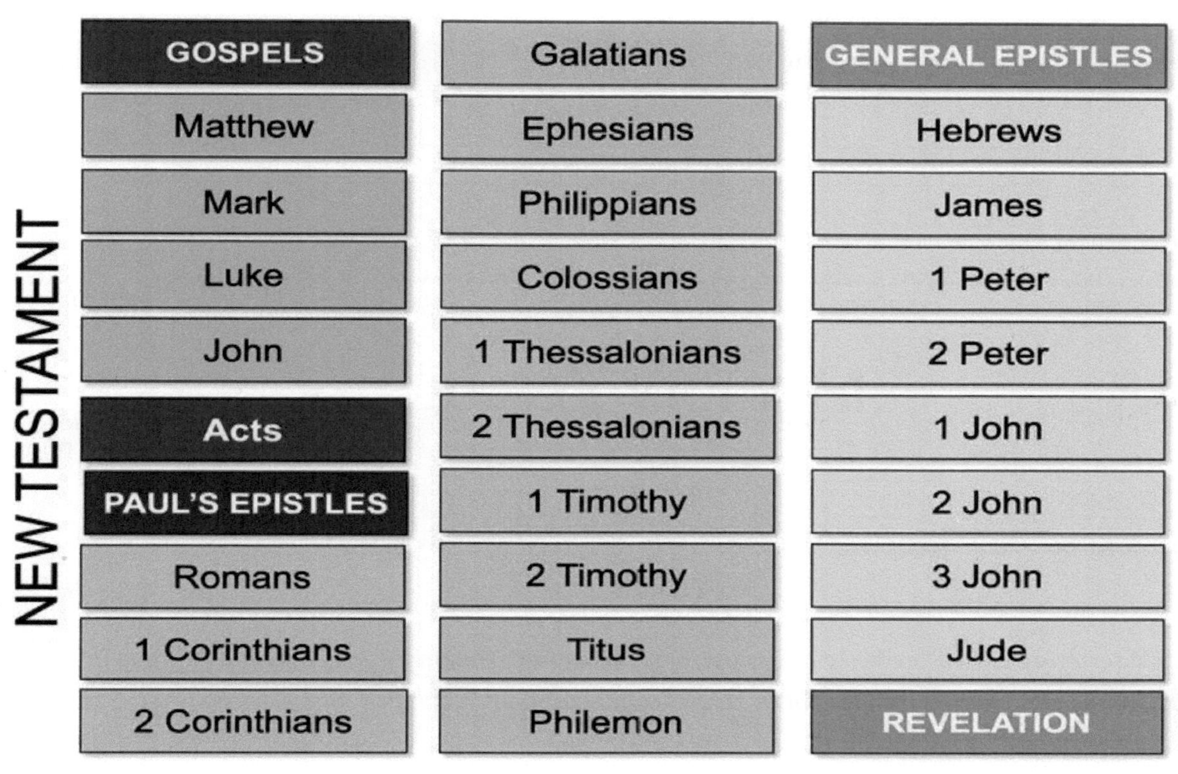

Source: Bible Layout

- What is Canon?

____

____

- Why did Bible pass through Canon?

____

____

- What are the different types books in the old testament?

____

- What are the different types books in the new testament?

- Discuss how and why you think Bible is so unique?

****

Memory Verse

****

2 Timothy 3:16-17

"All Scripture is God-breathed and is useful for teaching, rebuking, correcting and training in righteousness, so that the servant of God may be thoroughly equipped for every good work."

****

Christ Connect

****

"The stories in the Bible may be centuries ago but they provide insight and understanding to live a life of faith. Bible says the righteous shall live by faith (Romans 1:17).

Faith journey can be exciting and challenging at the same time, it may sound paradox, but the truth is those who have put their faith in the Lord Jesus will never be put to shame.

Ask the class members to come forward to share an experience which may have been challenging yet victorious!"

Make a book mark with the books of the Bible: firstly categorize it to 2 broad categories – Old and New testament. Then under the old write the 5 types of genres under each category. Based on the age group, this list can be expanded to include the books under each category. Color code the categories and the respective books.

Teacher/Student Notes Section

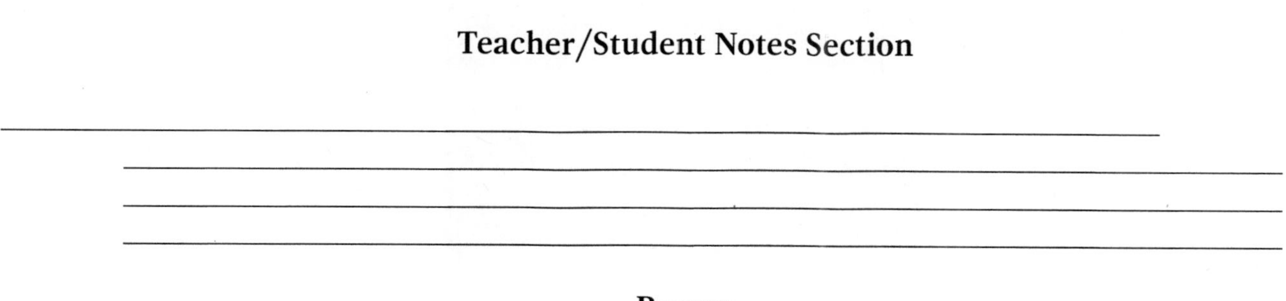

Prayer

Ask one of the children in the group if she/he would like to lead the class in prayer (to pray for their classmates, family, church, teachers and pastors, and on what they learnt).

CHAPTER TWO

God Created The World

Session Starter

Song: He's got the whole world in his hands

Genesis 1:1-23
(Encourage children to open their bibles to the story portion)

Explain

In the beginning, nothing existed except for God. God created everything. God spoke and created the heavens and the earth. When He first created the earth, it had no shape and total darkness covered the earth. The Spirit of God was hovering over the waters.

God spoke. He said, "Let there be light!" and what God said happened. The light was created. God saw that the light was good, and He separated the light from the darkness. God called the light day, and He called the darkness night. Evening came, and then morning came. That was the first day of creation.

God spoke again: "Let there be an expanse between the waters to separate them." What God said happened. He made a space between the water that was on the earth and the water above the earth. God called the expanse sky. Evening came, and then morning came. That was the second day of creation.

God said, "Let the water under the sky be gathered into one place, and let the dry land appear." What God said happened. God called the dry land earth, and He called the gathered water seas. God saw that it was good. Then God said, "Let the earth make plants and trees with fruits and seeds." What God said happened. Plants and trees grew, and God saw that it was good. Evening came, and then morning came. That was the third day of creation.

Next, God spoke to the light and separated the day from night. God created the sun to shine during the day and the moon and stars to shine at night. God gave us lights to provide light on the earth, to separate the day from night, and to help us track time in days and years. God saw that it was good. Evening came, and then morning came. That was the fourth day of creation.

Next, God said, "Let the water teem with living creatures, and let birds fly above the earth across the vault of the sky" and he made creatures that move and swim in the water. He made birds flap their wings and soar across the sky. God saw that it was good. God told the animals to multiply, and they filled the seas and the sky. Evening came, and then morning came. Then God made more animals—livestock, creatures that crawl, and wildlife to live on the earth. When God said it, it happened. And God saw that it was good. That was the fifth day of creation. Next class, we will see what God created on the sixth day.

****

Memory Verse

****

“Genesis 1:1
In the beginning God created the heavens and the earth.”

Blanco

****

Christ Connect

****

“The Bible says that, Jesus is Lord over all of creation. Everything was created by Him and for Him. The Son has always existed, and He holds everything together (Colossians 1:16 -17).”

Create a mini greenhouse and talk about God's creation and our responsibility to care for it.
You Will Need:

- coloured plastic cups
- clear plastic cups that are slightly smaller or larger than your coloured cups
- a push pin
- potting soil
- seeds (try to choose something with a short germination period)
- water

Instructions:

- Use the push pin to poke several holes in the bottom of your coloured cup. This will allow for some drainage, should your plants be overwatered.
- Fill your cup nearly to the top with potting soil and pat it down gently.
- Carefully place your seeds in your soil-filled cup, making sure to leave some space between each one. You can plant as few or as many as you like, but we usually use 3 - 5 seeds per greenhouse.
- Cover your seeds with an additional scoop of soil and once again, pat it down gently.
- Give your seeds some water.
- Place your clear cup over your solid-coloured cup to form a greenhouse.
- Add a little water every day or two and it won't be long before you see some little sprouts popping up. Good luck!

Teacher/Student Notes Section

____

____

____

____

Prayer

Ask one of the children in the group if she/he would like to lead the class in prayer (to pray for their classmates, family, church, teachers and pastors, and on what they learnt).

CHAPTER THREE

GOD CREATED MAN

Session Starter

Take a blank A3 size paper. Using a ink pad ask each child to press their thumb finger on to the ink pad (you can also use a graphite pencil to make thumb impression). Let each child put their name under their thumb impression. Let children wipe their hands with wet wipes to clean off any ink from the finger. Stick the sheet to the board and start with the class How God created Man in His own image from Genesis 1:26.

Genesis 1:1-24- 2:25
(Encourage children to open their bibles to the story portion)

Explain

Last week we heard the story of creations how God made: light on Day 1, water and sky on Day 2, land and plants on Day 3, Sun, moon and stars on Day 4, and birds, fish, and animals on Day 5... but the story of creation did not stop their ... God on Day 6 created some of the most beautiful creations, God said "Let the land produce living creatures according to their kinds: the livestock, the creatures that move along the ground, and the wild animals, each according to its kind." And it was so. 25 God made the wild animals according to their kinds, the livestock according to their kinds, and all the creatures that move along the ground according to their kinds. And God saw that it was good.

Today we are going to read from the Bible the most beautiful creation that happened on the sixth day of creation, God made man. God created people differently than anything else He created. God created people in His very own image. God took dust from the ground and made a man. God breathed His very own breath into the man, and the man became alive. God made a garden in the land of Eden, and He put the man in the garden. God told the man to work in the garden and take care of it. God provided food from the trees for the man to eat, and God provided a river to water the garden.

Then God said, "You can eat from any of the trees in the garden, except for one." The garden had a tree in it called the tree of the knowledge of good and evil. God warned the man, "If you eat from that tree, you will die." Now God was not yet finished with creation. He saw the man and said, "It is not good for the man to be alone." So God decided to make a helper for the man. God made wild animals and birds, and the man gave names to all of the creatures. But none of the animals was a good helper for the man. So God made the man fall fast asleep. He took one of the man's ribs and created a woman. When the man saw the woman, he was very happy.

The woman was the man's helpmate, and companion; she was his wife. The man's name was Adam, and his wife's name was Eve. God gave Adam and Eve good things. He put them in charge of the animals and provided everything they needed.

God looked at everything He had made, and it was very good. God was very happy with all the creations specially man (man includes male and female). And on the seventh day of creation, God rested from His work.

Show a video at the end of this class on Gods Creation, e.g., https://www.youtube.com/watch?v=ean_aMNkAgM

Apprehend

- From the story of creation from Genesis 1:1 – Gen 2:26, one specific word is emphasized in the process of creation, what is that word?

____

____

- What power had God given us with our tongue? There is a verse in proverbs which talks about the power of tongue. Try to find it out and write here. Explain how you can use your words with your friends and family carefully to build and not break.

____

____

****

Memory Verse

****

"Genesis 1:26

Then God said, "Let us make mankind in our image, in our likeness, so that they may rule over the fish in the sea and the birds in the sky, over the livestock and all the wild animals, and over all the creatures that move along the ground.""

****

Christ Connect

****

"God created man in His own image, and with authority. But, Adam lost his power and authority as sin entered. So, God sent His Son, Jesus, to reconcile us (restore) our relationship with God (Colossians 1:15). Jesus is the perfect representation of God because He is God (Hebrews 1:3)."

ACROSS

3) The ________ said to the woman, "Has God really said, 'You shall not eat of any tree of the garden?'" (Genesis 3:1 ESV)
6) "They sewed fig _____ together and made coverings..." (Genesis 3:7 ESV)
7) "God formed out of the ______ all the wild animals and birds in the sky." (Genesis 2:19 ESV)
9) Yah made Adam from the _____ of the earth. (Genesis 2:7 ESV)
10) Which book of the Bible tells the story of Adam & Eve?
12) God planted a garden in this place. (Genesis 2:8 ESV)

DOWN

1) "..she took some of its ______, and ate.." (Genesis 3:6 ESV)
2) "You may freely eat of every tree of the garden; but you shall not eat of the tree of the ________ of good and evil..." (Genesis 2:16-17 ESV)
4) Name of the first man. (Genesis 2:20 ESV)
5) Yah placed ________ at the east of the garden. (Genesis 3:24 ESV)
8) God made a woman from the ___ He took out of Adam. (Genesis 2:22 ESV)
11) Name of Adam's wife. (Genesis 3:20 ESV)

Source: https://biblepathwayadventures.com/activities/adam-eve/

Teacher/Student Notes Section

____

____

____

____

Prayer

Ask one of the children in the group if she/he would like to lead the class in prayer (to pray for their classmates, family, church, teachers and pastors, and on what they learnt).

CHAPTER FOUR

Sin Entered Mankind

Session Starter

Ask children if they ever had to face any consequence for a wrong choice, they made disobeying parents or elders. Play this video https://www.youtube.com/watch?v=ddbb6hlSsBE

After the video tell children that this is not myth or a fairy tale story, this is a real story that happened to mankind depicting the consequence of sin by first man and is written in the book of Genesis chapter 3.

Genesis 3:1-24.
(Encourage children to open their bibles to the story portion)

In our last class, we studied how God created light on Day 1, water & sky on Day2, land & plants on Day3, Sun, moon & stars on Day 4, birds & fish on Day 5, animals & mankind on Day 6. God created Adam, and then out of Adam's rib, he created Eve to be a suitable helpmate for Adam, and them together to subdue and have dominion over all God's creations.

God settled them under His presence in the garden of Eden. God commanded Adam that he could eat from any tree in the garden except for one. It was called the tree of the knowledge of good and evil. God said that if Adam did eat from the tree, he would die. (discuss examples when children are given all options except for some, yet the restricted thing is what they want... where did this nature come from, read on..). The Lord gave them only one restriction: "You must not eat from the tree of the knowledge of good and evil," and the punishment was severe: "You will certainly die" (Gen. 2:17). Though Adam and Eve could enjoy and eat from any other tree, that one tree which was restricted tempted them. They were enticed by the serpent (the devil). Eve believed the lies that the devil whispered into her ears that "you will not die" and she, in turn, influenced Adam to believe the lies.

Everything changed when Adam and Eve gave in to the serpent's temptation. The freedom and God's presence left when Adam and Eve sinned. Their eyes were opened, they were aware of their nakedness, and they felt ashamed. Surely the Lord's heart broke at their act of disobedience and rebellion. Because of their sin, He cast them out of the garden.

Though they did not die right away physically, the consequence of this sin was a spiritual death- the separation of God from man. Their lives and their children's lives—and the lives of all of mankind—were affected forever by their choice. But God did not leave Adam and Eve without hope. He promised that one of Eve's descendants would strike the head of the serpent (Gen.3:15) and crush the head of the snake and put an end to the curse over creation.

Sin is a big problem that needs a big solution. At just the right time, God sent His Son into the world, to save His people from their sins. Though the sin was bad news, we have the good news that: "Jesus Christ came into the world to save sinners" (1 Timothy 1:15) and set free those who were under the bondage of sin and law and be adopted as the Children of God.

- What does it meaan that man is made in the image of God?

____

- Are you tempted to sin against God in your everyday life? Discuss how the choices we make can have a eternal impact on our lives.

____

- Did Adam and Eve die, when they disobeyed God and ate the fruit from tree of knowledge of good and evil? How? Explain

____

____

****

Memory Verse

****

"Genesis 3:15
I will put enmity between you and the woman, and between your offspring and hers; he will crush your head, and you will strike his heel."

****

Christ Connect

****

"Adam and Eve sinned against God and sin entered mankind through one man. Our sin separates us from God. God promised that one of Eve's descendants would put an end to sin and death. When the right time came God sent His Son, Jesus into the world to rescue people from sin and bring them back to God to be children of God (Galatians 4:4). For as in Adam all die, so in Christ all will be made alive (1Corinthians 15:22)"

~

Do

Count the Cost

Below are some of the consequences of the Fall.
In the empty spaces write out some consequences of sin.

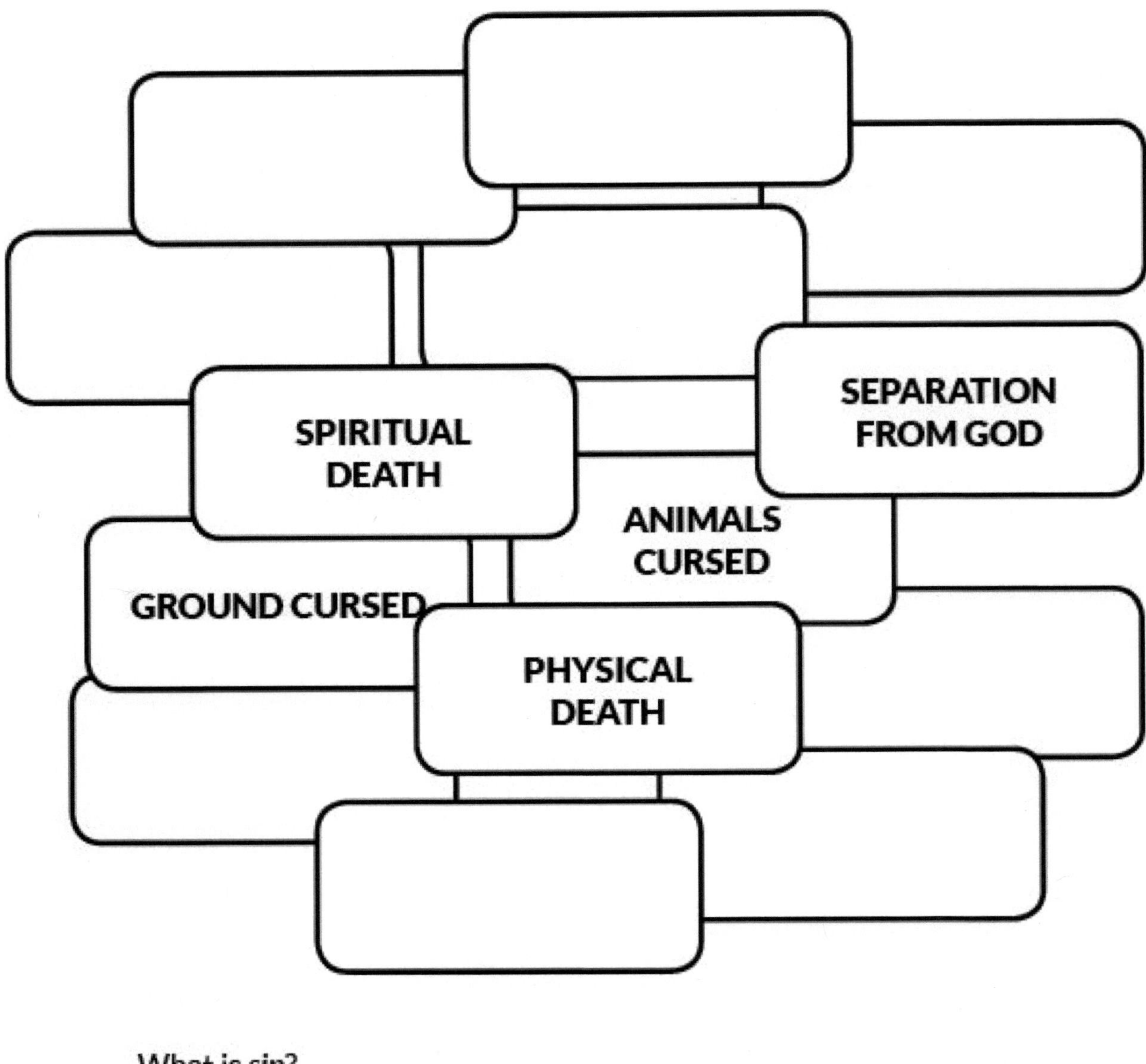

What is *sin*? ______________________________.

Adam and Eve's decision to eat from the tree was an attempt to take God off His throne as King and make themselves king instead.

Source: Activity Book. Generations of Grace

Teacher/Student Notes Section

____

____

____

____

Prayer

Ask one of the children in the group if she/he would like to lead the class in prayer (to pray for their classmates, family, church, teachers and pastors, and on what they learnt).

CHAPTER FIVE

THE FIRST BROTHERS

Session Starter

Some children may have one brother or one sister and some may have more than one (and some may not have siblings). Children, what is your family like, do you have any brothers or sisters? Today we are going to tell a Bible story about two brothers - in fact the first brothers.

Genesis 4:1-16,25-26.
(Encourage children to open their bibles to the story portion)

Explain

Do you remember Adam and Eve -the very first man and woman that God had created? Now they had two little boys. One brother was named Cain and one brother was named Abel. Imagine Adam and Eve's joy as their family grew. With each birth, maybe Eve hoped that this son would be the one to end the curse of sin, to crush the head of the snake (Gen. 3:15) (remember we learnt that in our last class), but the story of the first brothers was grievous and was an example of how sin affected their children.

When they were little Cain always liked playing in the dirt and trying to grow little gardens. Abel liked to play around with the sheep and goats that his father raised. When they were grown, Cain and Abel each had jobs. Abel was a shepherd, caring for his flocks of animals. Cain worked the ground as a farmer.

Once a year Adam and Eve and Cain and Abel would go to a place where they would make prayers to God and give God something that was special to them. This was the way they showed their love for God. It was called a "sacrifice." Abel took a perfect little lamb from his flock to offer to God. Abel was happy to give his lamb to God to show how much he loved God. Cain, however, wasn't very happy about giving anything to God.

God knows exactly how we feel and what we think when we give an offering or do anything for God. We may make many offerings and sacrifices to God, but God is always pleased with a cheerful giver. God knew that Cain's gift was not being offered out of love and God was not pleased with what Cain gave. God also knew what Abel felt and thought, and God knew Abel loved him and was happy about his gift. God accepted Abel's offering, but He did not accept Cain's. Cain was very angry! He was mad at Abel because God liked Abel's sacrifice best. God told Cain that if he did right and had good thoughts, his gift would be accepted, but Cain was still very mad.

Do you think God is happy when we get angry and kick things or throw things or yell bad names? No, God wants us to obey our parents and be kind and loving with our brothers and sisters and friends. But Cain was angry and hated Abel and he started thinking about ways to hurt Abel. This was very bad, wasn't it? We should never want to hurt someone else, and we shouldn't stay mad like Cain did. If you are mad at a brother or sister or friend what would be a good thing to do? If you give them a big hug and tell them you like them, they would be very happy and both of you would be friends again. This would please God too, isn't it? But Cain didn't try to please God or be kind to Abel.

God knew the intentions of Cain's heart. God warned Cain about sin, and told him what he needed to do to be accepted as we read in Genesis 4:6-7 "Then the Lord said to Cain, "Why are you angry? Why is your face downcast? 7 If you do what is right, will you not be accepted? But if you do not do what is right, sin is crouching at your door; it desires to have you, but you must rule over it." But Cain did not obey God. One day when Cain and Abel went out into the field, Cain took revenge and killed Abel. Then Cain hid Abel's body and pretended nothing had happened. Adam and Eve looked and looked for Abel but they didn't know what had happened to him. God knew what Cain did, and God called to Cain, "Where is Abel?" God asked. Cain said, "I don't know!"

God punished Cain and cursed him as we read in Genesis 4:11-12, "Now you are under a curse and driven from the ground, which opened its mouth to receive your brother's blood from your hand. When you work the ground, it will no longer yield its crops for you. You will be a restless wanderer on the earth." Cain didn't ask God to forgive him, instead, he ran away from home and he wouldn't go to pray to God anymore. God sent Cain away from the land to wander the earth. Cain's sin separated him from God and people.

Adam and Eve were very sad as they had lost both their children - Abel was killed and Cain was wandering away from God. One day God told them that he would give them a new baby boy to make them happy again. This boy was named Seth. Seth was a very good little boy and as he grew up, he gave Adam and Eve much happiness. Seth loved God and tried to do good things to please God all his life. Seth was not the Promised One either, but Jesus would come from Seth's descendants. (See Luke 3:23-38.)

Since the fall of Adam and Eve, sin entered mankind. Sin always tries to crouch through our door to tempt us and make us disobey God. Studying the word of God, understanding him will help us to live a life pleasing to God and not fall prey to sin.

In Genesis 4:7 we read, "If you do what is right, will you not be accepted? But if you do not do what is right, sin is crouching at your door; it desires to have you, but you must rule over it." Explain this verse in context to your everyday schooling, family and friends. Discuss with your group and write your answer.

****

Memory Verse

****

"Genesis 4:7
If you do what is right, will you not be accepted? But if you do not do what is right, sin is crouching at your door; it desires to have you, but you must rule over it."
"

Blanco

****

****

"Adam and Eve sinned against God and since then every man is born in sin, sin had entered mankind. Generation after generation, God's people lived with an expectant hope of a redeemer to save them from sin. Jesus came as a propitiation of the sin to save us from eternal death...just as sin entered the world through one person Adam, salvation also entered the world through one person Jesus Christ, and just as Adam brought death to all who followed him, Christ brought life to all who follow him (Romans 5:12)."

```
P K M A R K R N F R A H I T L
U H I Z X E T I E I B C L O Y
N C Z L L H R S K L E C R P F
I O X L L S P D E R L D E S R
S V I U T E E Z E Q S N R K U
H T Y B C S D F P I F E I Z I
M N O T R M Q N E J H U E O T
E R E U A X V X R T Q K V V Y
N D C I D I U A O L V S E L P
T J A J A V G R F J M U A C D
P L E L M N B D S V R N K F D
O F F E R I N G H R B E Q I A
H D M M E A B P E R I S Y E W
A N G R Y C D U E K U N R L Z
K R X P C M O K P J Q T M D C
```

ABEL
ADAM
ANGRY
BROTHERS
CAIN
CURSED
EVE
FIELD
FIRSTBORN
FRUIT
KEEPER OF SHEEP
KILLED
LORD
MARK
OFFERING
PUNISHMENT
RESPECTED
TILLER

Source: http://www.joyfulmeditations.org/downloads/kids/worksheets/calvarychapel/en/ot/curr005.pdf

Teacher/Student Notes Section

Prayer

Ask one of the children in the group if she/he would like to lead the class in prayer (to pray for their classmates, family, church, teachers and pastors, and on what they learnt).

CHAPTER SIX

THE FIRST FLOOD

Session Starter

Are you all ready for a story! ... so here we go ... once there was a young boy who was bored living in his countryside house with his parents though, he had everything and more than he wanted, he was not happy. One day he left his home and parents to go to the city to have fun and enjoy his life but once he got away from his father and mother and family .. his life became very hard. There was no one to keep him safe, or give him food, or love him. So, "This is like people when they try to live without God". In our lesson today we will learn more about what happened when people first started rejecting God."

Read Genesis 6:9-21
(Encourage children to open their bibles to the story portion. Teachers can summarize verses from Genesis 6:5 - 9:17, while explaining)

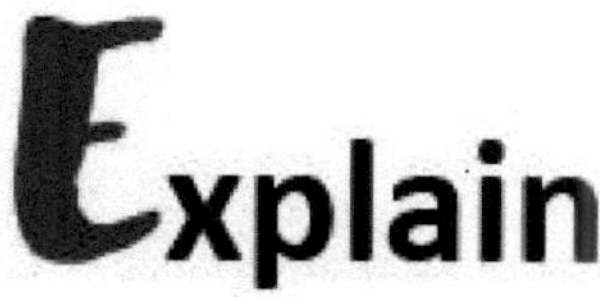

How many of you have heard about Flood? Flood brings in the sense of destruction, loss and trauma. After humans rejected God as their king, the world became a terrible place to live. This lesson deals with the consequences of the fall which came in the form of flood, as God's judgment upon sin.

God's judgment is his good and right punishment for our sins. God's own creation- mankind were fighting against God. It was good and right for God to unmake everything that he had made because it was fighting against him. But we can see God's love in his saving Noah and his family.

In Noah's time it did not rain. Ever! There was also no such thing as an umbrella because, up until that point, there was no rain! No weather forecast of rains or any such thing ...in such a time God decided to send rain on earth as a judgement. The whole Earth would be covered with water, and all life on Earth would die - except for Noah and family whom God found righteous. God told Noah about his plan to flood the earth. And God told Noah to build an ark for him and his family as we read in Genesis 6:17-20 "I am going to bring floodwaters on the earth to destroy all life under the heavens, every creature that has the breath of life in it. Everything on earth will perish. 18 But I will establish my covenant with you, and you will enter the ark—you and your sons and your wife and your sons' wives with you. 19 You are to bring into the ark two of all living creatures, male and female, to keep them alive with you. 20 Two of every kind...."

God gave Noah the exact dimensions for the ark. Once again, no one had ever seen a flood, so no one could imagine such a thing happening. Yet Noah didn't hesitate when God told him to build an ark. Noah went to work. He recruited his sons, and they started chopping wood. For more than a century – that's a hundred years! - Noah and his sons worked on the ark. It must have looked funny for Noah's neighbors and people who saw Noah and his sons working on the ark... they must have thought this man is crazy to build a giant boat. They must have teased and joked on Noah.. But as we read, God was not joking about the rain and the flood. God told Noah and his children, and two of every living thing (male and female) that moved on land—birds, livestock, wild animals, all the creatures that swarm over the earth, and all mankind to enter the ark in pairs, male and female.

Then the flood came, as God promised, we read in Genesis 7:11-12, "11 In the six hundredth year of Noah's life, on the seventeenth day of the second month—on that day all the springs of the great deep burst forth, and the floodgates of the heavens were opened. 12 And rain fell on the earth forty days and forty nights."

The waters rose and increased greatly on the earth, and the ark floated on the surface of the water. Every living thing that moved on land perished—birds, livestock, wild animals, all the creatures that swarm over the earth, and all mankind. Everything on dry land that had the breath of life in its nostrils died. Every living thing on the face of the earth was wiped out; people and animals and the creatures that move along the ground and the birds were wiped from the earth. The waters flooded the earth for a hundred and fifty days (about 5 months!!). Only Noah was left, and those with him in the ark. God remembered Noah and all the wild animals and the livestock that were with him in the ark, and he sent a wind over the earth, and the waters receded.

By the 27th day of the first month of Noah's 601st year (almost a year after), the water dried up and the earth was completely dry. Then Noah came out of the ark with his wife and his sons and their wives, and all the living creature that was with them in the ark—God blessed Noah to "multiply on the earth and be fruitful and increase in number" (Genesis 9:1) and gave them commands to live on the clean earth, starting life again on earth!

God made a rainbow covenant with Noah, as we read in Genesis 9:13-15, "13 I have set my rainbow in the clouds, and it will be the sign of the covenant between me and the earth. 14 Whenever I bring clouds over the earth and the rainbow appears in the clouds, 15 I will remember my covenant between me and you and all living creatures of every kind. Never again will the waters become a flood to destroy all life."

It took a great deal of faith for Noah to build that ark, but because Noah had faith, he ignored the laughter and mocking of his neighbors, and he finished what he started. It's not always easy to do the right thing. We live in a world a lot like Noah's world, many do not believe in God like we do, and when we tell them we need to obey God, they might laugh at us. There's only one way to counter the criticism of the world, and that's faith.

Faith is believing in things we cannot see with our eyes (Hebrews 11:1). We can't see oxygen, but when we breathe in, we have faith that it's there because it's always been there. Noah had faith in God because he had a relationship with God. He had never seen God's face, but he knew God through his voice and through his creation. Noah knew God well enough to trust him when God said there would be a flood. For Noah it was the same as breathing in. God had always been there for him, and he knew God would not let him down.

- God found Noah blameless and righteous and preserved him and his family while he wiped all mankind and creatures – as a judgement for wrongdoing. Discuss with your group, how man take God for granted and take his commands lightly under this age of grace.

____

____

- What do you think will their be consequences for such actions?

____

____

****

Memory Verse

****

Genesis 6:9,13,18

"Noah was a righteous man, blameless among the people of his time, and he walked faithfully with God....13 ..God said to Noah... 18 ... I will establish my covenant with you, and you will enter the ark..."

Blanco

****

Christ Connect

****

"God rescued Noah and his family from the flood; only they lived. The story of Noah points us to God's Son, Jesus—the only perfectly righteous One— who came to take the punishment for our sin. By trusting in Him, we are saved from the punishment our sin deserves. Jesus died so that we can live.... In 2Corinthians 5:21, it is written, "God made him who had no sin to be sin for us, so that in him we might become the righteousness of God".. By believing and putting our faith in Jesus .. we are saved."

Blanco

Build an Ark

Different age groups can divide the parts and collate all together in a single board

Materials:

1. White posterboard
2. Crayons
3. Toothpicks or craft sticks
4. Animal crackers
5. Cotton balls
6. Silver tinsel
7. Feathers
8. Green chenille stem
9. Any other color chenille stem
10. 1 in. wide ribbon 1 yard long

Directions:

1) Cut 5 3 in. circles from white posterboard. One set for each child.

2) On the first circle, have the children make an ark out of toothpicks or craft sticks broken into shorter pieces. Depending on your age group you may have to draw the shape and have them fill in with the chosen material. also have them color the background to look like hills, sky etc.

3) On the next circle, have them draw the background again and then glue animal crackers in matching pairs.

4) On the 3rd circle, have them glue cotton balls for clouds and silver tinsel for the rain.

5) On the 4th circle, draw a bird head and have them glue on feathers. Take a green chenille stem and bend it into two loops to look like leaves and glue to the bird's mouth (the dove returning with the olive branch).

6) Have the children draw a rainbow. You could also use scraps of tissue paper for them to glue on for the rainbow.

7) Glue the circles in order onto wide ribbon. You may want to put a Bible verse on an index card at the bottom such as Gen 9:13 "I set my rainbow in the cloud, and it shall be a promise between Me and the earth."

8) For a hanger, bend a chenile stem in half and then twist and bend into a circle, then fold the top of the ribbon over and glue around the circle. I also cut a V-shape out of the bottom of the ribbon to give it a finished look.

Source: https://www.childfun.com/themes/christian/noahs-ark/

Teacher/Student Notes Section

Prayer

Ask one of the children in the group if she/he would like to lead the class in prayer (to pray for their classmates, family, church, teachers and pastors, and on what they learnt).

CHAPTER SEVEN

THE TOWER OF BABEL

Session Starter

Welcome children with "hello" in different languages. (Spanish: "Hola!"; French: "Bonjour!"; Swahili: "Hujambo"). Ask them if they know to say "hello".. in other Indian, Chinese, Arabic or other languages......In today's Bible story, we are going to see where and how people suddenly started speaking in so many different languages!

Read Genesis 11:1-9.
(Encourage children to open their bibles to the story portion)

After the great flood, God told Noah and his sons to grow their families and fill the earth. Noah's sons got married and had children. Their families grew, and the people started to travel through the land. At this time, everyone in the world spoke the same language. One day, the people travelled through a valley. They liked it there, and they decided to live there.

"We don't want to be scattered all over the earth," they said. "Let's build a city and a tower so big that it touches the sky. The tower will make us famous!" The people were not doing what God had told them to do. They wanted to be as important as God. They were saying "Look how great we are," instead of "Look how great God is." They wanted glory for themselves instead of God. But God is greater than anyone. God created people to give glory to Him alone.

The people made bricks out of clay and baked them in the fire to make stones. Then they used the stones to start building the tower. God came down to look at the tower. God said, "If they are doing this, they will keep thinking up more bad things to do. We need to stop them." So God mixed up the people's words. Instead of everyone speaking the same language, everyone spoke different languages.

Can you imagine how hard it would be to build a tower without being able to speak the same language? The people had to stop building the tower. Families had to move away from each other to live with people they could understand. Not only did God confuse their language but he also scattered the people all over the earth. Now there were groups of people in different places all over the world. God could see how prideful the people's hearts were becoming and he put a stop to it. God knew that if he didn't discipline his people, they would fall deeper and deeper into sin. That's not what God wants! He wants us to know him and glorify Him because only he is worthy of all glory.

The people were scattered all over the world- just what God had told them to do after the flood (ask children the covenant God had made with Noah after the flood). The city with the unfinished tower was called Babel.

God punished the people for their pride. He confused their language so they couldn't understand each other, and they were scattered all over the earth. Had God told them to spread across the world? (Remind children of the covenant God had made with Noah after the flood). When man glorifies himself, God will humble man, because only God is worthy of worship and praise!

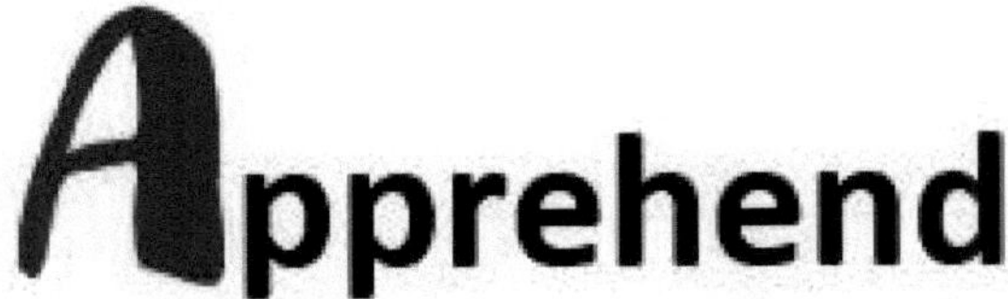

- What does the word "Glorify" means?

  ____
  ____

- What does it mean to glorify God?

  ____
  ____

- What does it look like when people glorify themselves instead of God?

  ____
  ____

- Discuss with children how in today's world we see and hear a lot of self-glorification. How do you think, God looks at it.

  ____
  ____

- Self- introspect- Let each child self introspect in their everyday lives and see how they could change in a way that their life would glorify God than man.

  ____
  ____

****

Memory Verse

****

"Colossians 3:17
And whatever you do, whether in word or deed, do it all in the name of the Lord Jesus, giving thanks to God the Father through him."

Blanco

****

****

"All the people was spread over the whole earth and they couldn't understand each other anymore. That's how it still is today. There are thousands of languages spoken in hundreds of countries all over the world! But we read something really exciting in Revelation 7:9. (apostle John writes) "I looked and there before me was a great multitude that no one could count, from every nation, tribe, people and language, standing before the throne and in front of the Lamb." Even though we all speak different languages now, there will be people who are worshipping Jesus in heaven from all over the world! We might all look and sound different, but we will all be worshipping the same great God and glorifying God for HE alone is worthy of all glory and honor (Revelation 4:11)."

Do

WORD SEARCH

TOWER OF BABEL

```
N N D M O U D Z B I T U M E N E A Z O F
V H D O T R S T O N E L O U R K K R J V
R T W R R N F C S H N T O E W V V R H R
E L L T R I O O S K P N Q O R X Z I S W
Y W A A M E Q K W C A L Z X Q B V W V D
I T H R N C K S D L B P R U M I H E V O
O K Z X R G Y A P E O P L E X B E S C A
Y M C I T Y U H I Q T O Y R K L A U D W
G J C E G M Z A Q O P D E N G E V A Z L
T S C A L Z F N G G D M N B S Y E H R M
Y O T E P Z I U A E I U L R W J N P I D
H Z R O H M C P V X E L R F B J S H G Q
W S C A T T E R E D G N C J Q A G U M C
H V A W H N A L S T J E B N L Y B H T K
K A X P D F Y C F M B R I C K M T E U E
M Q P W Q P C G S R M T K V D D O R L A
S P E E C H Q F I S H I N A R O W J P R
R B I M B O Y B O W O X M T J K E T R T
N O F R Y G T T T Z B C N Y T E R Q Z H
E H C O N F U S I O N J V T Q N I Q R B
```

CONFUSION	BITUMEN	PEOPLE
SPEECH	SHINAR	BABEL
CITY	YHWH	SCATTERED
LANGUAGE	BIBLE	HEAVENS
EARTH	TOWER	BRICK
TORAH	STONE	MORTAR

For more free Bible resources and Teacher Packs including coloring pages, worksheets, quizzes and more visit our website at: www.biblepathwayadventures.com

Teacher/Student Notes Section

Prayer

Ask one of the children in the group if she/he would like to lead the class in prayer (to pray for their classmates, family, church, teachers and pastors, and on what they learnt).

CHAPTER EIGHT

God's Covenant with Abraham

Session Starter

Abraham is going to leave Haran and is never coming back. He has to take everything he owns with him on the journey. He does not know where he is going to go or the weather in that place. Go back in time and make a list of all the things he might have needed at that time, also keep in mind their mode of travel. Talk about how easy or difficult or easy would it have been?

Genesis 12:1-3, 15:1-21, and 17:1-9.
(Encourage children to open their bibles to the story portion. Teachers can summarize selected portions from Genesis 12, 15 and 17 while explaining).

Noah's son Shem had a family. Shem's seventh-great grandson was named Abram. God called Abram to leave behind his family and his lands to go to a place God would show him. So, he took all his possessions that he had with him set out as the Lord had directed him to. Abram travelled toward the land of Canaan with his wife, Sarai; his father, Terah; and his nephew, Lot. But they stopped in Haran and settled there. God chose Abram and told him to move to a place he had never been.

God had promised Abram three things: a large nation will make your name great and that he would bless those who bless him. The Lord did what he promised to Abram, he made Abram a large nation with his descendants, made his name great. Then Abram had to go to Egypt as there was a severe famine in the Land and had the fear of life and did not trust enough in the Lord and came up with his plan- to have Sarai tell others that he is her brother. Though it was a half-truth, yet it was a full lie. He was treated well for Sarai's sake by the Pharaoh and his officials. The Lord inflicted serious diseases on Pharaoh and his household and then Pharaoh sent Abram away with his wife, men and everything he had.

Abram moved to the Negev from Egypt. He was wealthy in livestock, in silver and gold. He came back to the same place (Bethel) where he had made an altar for the Lord earlier. A conflict arose between the herdsmen of Lot and Abram as the Land couldn't support them together. Abram let Lot choose which side he wanted to go with. Abram said if he wanted to go right, he would go left. Lot looked up and saw that the whole plain of Jordan was well-watered and Lot moved there and lived near Sodom. After Lot had moved away from Abram the Lord said "Lift up your eyes from where you are and look north and south and east and west and all the land that you see I will give you and your offspring". I will make your offspring like the dust of the earth.

There were 4 kings who took all the goods from Sodom and Gomorrah along with Lot and his possessions. Abram was not only Lot's uncle but also a good friend. As soon as he heard that Lot had been captured, he jumped into action. Abram took with him 318 trained men, risking his life travelled up to Dan (which is a long-distance) recovered goods and brought back Lot. We also know that Abram had military wisdom when he planned night attacks and he split them up into two groups. When Melchizedek King of Salem brought bread and wine, Abram gave him a tenth of everything. Abram rightfully returned everything that was plundered to the King of Sodom even though he asked Abram to keep the goods and return only the people. Abram told him that he does not want to keep the plunder and returned everything to the King but did not impose his principles on his allies and gave them their share instead.

God appeared to Abram in a vision and said "Don't be afraid Abram, I am your shield and your very great reward" Abram had his doubts, he was blessed materially but had no children. Abram asked the Lord if Eliezer was going to be his successor. The Lord told him Eliezer will not be his heir but he will have someone from his lineage. The Lord then took him out and had him see all the stars and mentioned to him that if anyone could count the stars then they could count his offspring. Abram believed and it was credited to him as righteousness. Abram boldly asks proof of promise to the Lord and the Lord asks him for a three-year-old heifer, a female goat, ram, turtle dove, young pigeon and he had cut them into half and lay them on the ground. A smoking pot and a blazing torch appeared and passed between the pieces which confirmed that the Lord made a covenant with Abram.

Sarai had an Egyptian maidservant named Hagar and Sarai wanted Abram to have children through her and Abram agreed. And when Hagar became pregnant, she despised her mistress. Then she went to Abram and said that "You are responsible for the wrong I am suffering" Abram responded to that by saying "Your servant is in your hands, do whatever you think is best". So, Sarai mistreated Hagar and she ran away from her and the angel of the Lord told her to go back to her mistress and submit to her.

When Abram was 99 years old, he was still childless. God appeared before him and said, if you walk before me and be blameless and that he would confirm his covenant and would increase his numbers. God said you will be called as the father of many nations and you will no longer be called Abram, your name will be called Abraham. He said that he would make him fruitful and make him a great nation.

Abram did not have any idea, where the Lord asked him to go. He did not know anything about the land. He did not know the weather, what kind of people were living there or any additional information he needed. He simply walked where the Lord wanted him to go!

God also gave Abram the promise that he would bless him and make his family so big and make them a big nation. God also said that all the people on the earth will be blessed through you. Wow!! What a big promise, but Abram was 75 years old and his wife Sarai did not have any children. Abram would have been confused as to how God is going to fulfil the promise.

Can you imagine if God asked you to leave behind everything you have and go to a foreign country where you do not know anyone or have any friends. Think about moving to a new school or a new community, how would you feel? How do you think you would respond to God?

Abram knew that the Lord had promised him the Land, but did not show any attitude or pride and generously lets Lot chose his share and then takes what he did not. How would you react? ***Abraham was not a perfect man, but God had a very special plan for his life. God also has a special plan for your life, what plan do you think God has for you in your life?***

****

Memory Verse

****

"Genesis 12:2-3
I will make you into a great nation, and I will bless you, I will make your name great, and you will be a blessing. I will bless those who bless you, and whoever curses you I will curse."

Blanco

****

Christ Connect

****

"God gave Abram many promises and chose him to be the Father of the Multitude and he will use us too if we are willing to trust and obey him. God is willing to forgive us, in spite of our mistakes, guide us through difficult circumstances and use us. Jesus died for our sins and he wants us to repent and trust in Christ. Jesus gave up everything he had in heaven to come to earth and save us from our sins. Jesus even gave up his own life, died on the cross in our place. God takes care of his children and those who believe in him."

Blanco

God Made a Promise to Abraham Word Search

Find the words on the list that are hidden in the puzzle. The words can be left to right, up and down, or diagonally.

I	T	N	H	J	A	T	B	H	E	S	I	S
T	I	O	C	A	N	A	A	N	A	T	V	E
L	A	I	Q	U	N	O	R	E	W	A	R	D
O	F	F	S	P	R	I	N	G	L	R	Q	B
Z	R	I	T	E	U	F	G	F	I	S	V	E
C	A	O	A	B	R	A	H	A	M	T	E	L
S	O	M	E	N	D	R	E	T	A	T	V	I
L	I	V	I	T	L	L	A	H	A	C	I	E
U	N	T	E	L	I	A	T	E	E	R	I	V
L	O	R	E	N	S	S	A	R	A	H	T	E
N	U	L	L	A	A	C	O	E	Q	U	I	D
N	O	N	S	E	Q	N	I	S	L	L	A	N
G	R	E	A	T	L	E	T	E	R	I	U	R

ABRAHAM	FATHER	OFFSPRING
BELIEVED	GREAT	STARS
CANAAN	REWARD	
COVENANT	SARAH	

Source: https://sundayschoolzone.com/activity/god-promised-abraham-word-search/

Teacher/Student Notes Section

____

____

____

____

Prayer

Ask one of the children in the group if she/he would like to lead the class in prayer (to pray for their classmates, family, church, teachers and pastors, and on what they learnt).

CHAPTER NINE

GOD TEST'S ABRAHAM

Session Starter

Show your children, rectangles of different sizes and ask them to make a tower- draw it may be. Then ask them why they put the biggest one on the bottom. You can talk about how well the large rectangle would keep the structure stable and would help it to hold the tower together. Relate the large rectangle to God (he is the foundation) and how Abraham had to make an important decision in his life, to choose what had to be first in his life.

Genesis 22:1-19
(Encourage children to open their bibles to the story portion)

Do you remember what God promised Abraham and Sarah? that they would have more children than anybody could count—as many as the stars in the sky! But they didn't have any children for a long time and were very old when God gave them a son. They named him Isaac. Since all of the people on earth would be blessed because of Abraham and Sarah's family, their son Isaac was very, very special.

Abraham blindly obeyed God before the birth of his son Isaac, later God tested Abraham to know if Abraham changed priorities after the birth of Isaac. God told Abraham to do something that sounded strange. God told Abraham to take Isaac to a special mountain and offer him to God. Long ago, in Bible times, people gave offerings to God as a token of love, to thank Him for something, or to say to God "I'm sorry; please forgive me." These offerings were called sacrifices. When the offering was an animal, then it was killed during sacrifice. People offered God the best animal from their flocks. This time, though, God didn't ask for an animal. He told Abraham to give his son Isaac as a sacrifice. Abraham loved Isaac very much. God had promised that Isaac would have a family. How could that happen if Abraham gave Isaac as a sacrifice? Abraham believed that God would make things turn out right. He did not know how God would do it, but Abraham believed God would keep His promise. So, Abraham obeyed God.

Early in the morning, Abraham, Isaac, and two helpers took a donkey and the supplies they needed. They travelled for three days until they came to the place God had told Abraham about. Then Abraham and Isaac went by themselves up the mountain. "Where is the lamb to sacrifice to God?" asked Isaac. Abraham said, "God will give us a lamb to sacrifice." Abraham built the altar- arranged the wood, tied up his son and laid him on the top of the wood. Then he reached out his hand and took the knife to slay his son. But heard a voice, called to them from heaven and said, "Abraham, I see that you were willing to do what I said. You do not have to offer your son Isaac." Abraham looked up and saw a fine sheep caught in the bushes. God had sent a lamb to sacrifice instead of Isaac. God, Abraham, and Isaac could see that Abraham loved God most of all. God said to Abraham, "You will have as many descendants as the stars in the sky and the sand on the seashore. All the world will be blessed because you have obeyed me."

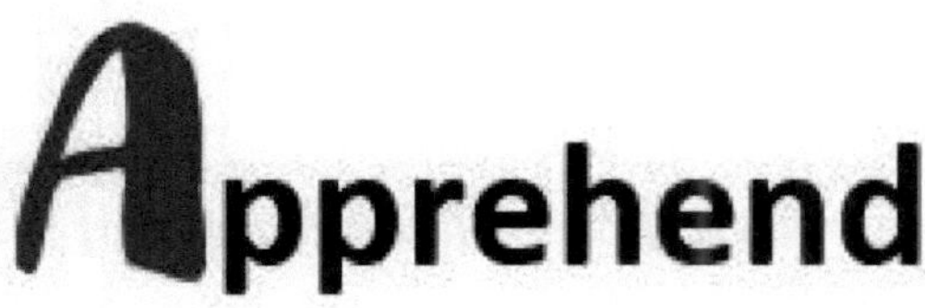

God promised Abraham, but had him wait for a long time before he provided what he promised. Abraham instantly obeyed God without any second thoughts. He did not discuss with his family or friends but plainly trusted God. ***Why would God grant him a son and then ask him to give it? He wanted to know if Abraham would believe him and that if he would trust and obey him unconditionally- When God wants to test us, he wants us to deepen our faith***

Abraham gave God the first place in his life. What about you? Is there anything in your life that God has blessed you with and has become more precious in your life? Are you making an idol out of something that God gave you as a gift? ***What would you do if your favourite TV program came in the same time as worship time? Would you let other things take the first place in your life?***

Do you have something in your life that is more important than God? A sport, game, friends, technology, family? Have a discussion about things that people love more than God.

****

****

“Genesis 15:6

Abram believed the Lord, and he credited it to him as righteousness.

”

****

Christ Connect

****

“While Abraham was spared having to sacrifice his son Isaac, the son of promise, God would not spare Himself. God willingly sacrificed His one and only Son to redeem people from their choice to sin. Sin separates us from God and deserves God's punishment of death (Romans 6:23). God the Father sent His Son Jesus, the perfect solution to our sins, to rescue us from the punishment we deserve. It's something we, as sinners, could never earn on our own. Jesus alone can save us. Jesus lived a perfect life, died on the cross for our sins, and rose again. Because Jesus gave up His life for us, we can be welcomed into God's family for eternity. This is the best gift that we can ever get! Believe in your heart that Jesus alone saves you through what He's already done on the cross. Repent, turn away from sin towards Jesus. Tell God and others!!”

Blanco

Do

Ask children to draw four squares on a piece (or fold the paper into 4 smaller squares). In one square they should write the word "GOD". In each of the other four squares they can draw pictures of people or things that are very important to them. Give them a sticker which they need to place in the square which they think deserves the first place in their life. Remember the word, seek ye first the kingdom of God. Are you giving God the first priority in your life?

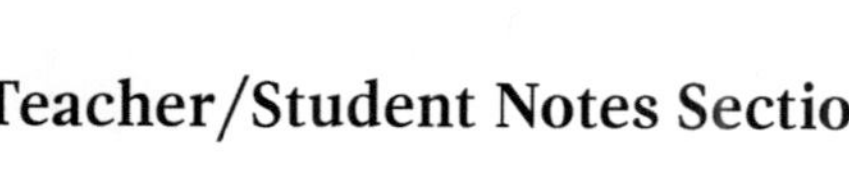

Teacher/Student Notes Section

____

____

____

____

Prayer

Ask one of the children in the group if she/he would like to lead the class in prayer (to pray for their classmates, family, church, teachers and pastors, and on what they learnt).

CHAPTER TEN

God Reaffirms His Promise To Abraham

Session Starter

Bring a few Hotwheel cars to the class, ask the kids to race and see who wins, now tell the kids, that they can use any kind of tricks to win. See what kind of strategies they use.

Genesis 25:19-26; 26:1-6; 28:10-22.
(Encourage children to open their bibles to the story portion)

Abraham became the father of Isaac and when Isaac was 40 years old when he married Rebekah who was the daughter of Bethuel and the sister of Laban. When Isaac prayed to the Lord on the behalf of his wife and the Lord answered his prayer by blessing them with twin boys. Esau the elder one was a skilful hunter while Jacob was a quiet man staying among the tents. Once when Jacob was cooking some stew, Esau came back from hunting, he was so hungry and he asked for some stew, to which Jacob said give me your birthright in return. This is how Esau despised his birthright.

There was a famine in the land and the Lord had appeared to Isaac and told him to not go to Egypt and asked him to stay there for a while and that God will be with him and bless him. The Lord also reminded him what he swore to Abraham about making his descendants as numerous as the stars. Isaac stayed in Gerar where God asked him to. Isaac planted crops in the land and reaped a hundredfold and his wealth continued to increase in the midst of famine.

When Isaac was old and his eyes were so weak that could no longer see, he called his older son Esau and told him to hunt and then prepare tasty food so he can eat it and bless him. When Rebekah overheard him, she had Isaac get some young goat from their flocks and she prepared it for Isaac. She also got him to wear Esau's clothes and tricked Isaac and took all of his blessings. When Esau realized that Jacob had stolen his blessings, he was so angry and wanted to kill him. So, Rebekah sent Jacob to his brother's house.

On his way to his uncle's house, he stopped for a night where he slept with a stone under his head. He had a dream where he saw a stairway resting on the earth and it's top reaching heaven and the angels of God ascending and descending on it and God standing on the top and saying that "I am the Lord, the God of your father Abraham and the God of Isaac. I will give you and your descendants the land on which you are lying. All people on the earth will be blessed through you, I will be with you and watch over you wherever you go and will bring you back to the land. I will not leave you until I have done what I have promised you".

When Jacob awoke from his sleep, he said surely God is in this place and that this is the house of God; the gate of heaven. Early the next day morning, Jacob took the stone he placed under his head and set it up as a pillar and poured oil on top. He called the place Bethel and made a vow for God that day saying "If God will be with me and watch over me on this journey I am taking and will give me food to eat and clothes to wear so that I return safely to my father's house then the Lord will be my God".

Jacob made a lot of choices in his life. A few good and a few bad ones. He faced the consequence of every choice that he made. We need to know that every choice we make and its outcome affects us and others in the future. ***What we choose and what we do determines the next step in our lives.*** Is it possible to make the right choice always? What would you do when you make a wrong choice? We all make wrong choices sometimes. Understand that anyone can make a mistake. Always think before you make a choice. Consciously make a choice that God wants you to make or will be proud. ***Talk about a time you had a choice and what you chose.***

****

Memory Verse

****

"*Genesis 28:15*

I am with you and will watch over you wherever you go, and I will bring you back to this land. I will not leave you until I have done what I have promised you."

****

Christ Connect

****

"***We are all like Jacob, we are sinners (we lie, deceive, scheme, manipulate) and we are wholly undeserving to receive the blessing of God almighty. Like Jacob we can enter into a relationship with Christ today by asking forgiveness for our sine and declaring God to be our saviour and Redeemer. By admitting our faults to Him, God can give us a new life, and we can enter into an eternal relationship with Him. Jacob was able to experience a new identity through his new name, Israel. In the same way, when we come to know Christ, we experience a transformation. It changes everything: our lives, our thoughts, our actions, etc.***"

Do

Have a discussion in class about different characteristics and everything you know about Jacob, Esau, Isaac and Rebekah- an example has been given. Make a similar chart per your discussion, and you can even stick it on top the sample given!

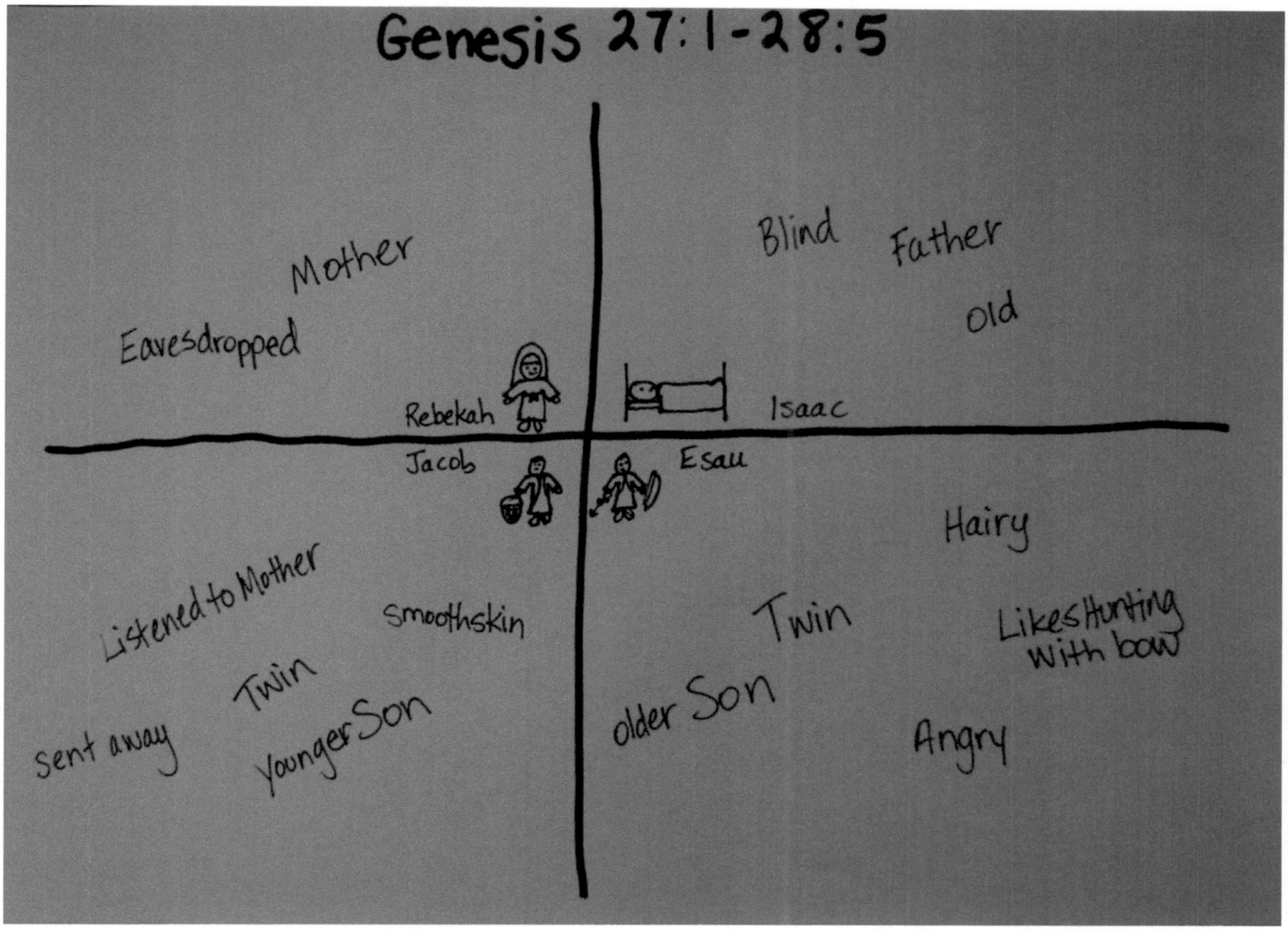

Genesis 27:1-28:5

Mother
Eavesdropped
Rebekah
Blind
Father
Old
Isaac
Jacob
Esau
Listened to Mother
Smoothskin
Twin
Younger Son
Sent away
Hairy
Twin
Likes Hunting with bow
older Son
Angry

Source: https://i1.wp.com/missionbibleclass.org/wp-content/uploads/2015/05/img_9439.jpg?ssl=1

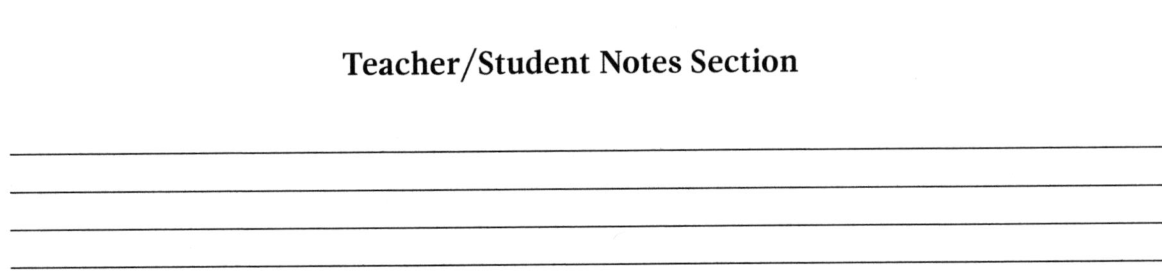

Teacher/Student Notes Section

Prayer

Ask one of the children in the group if she/he would like to lead the class in prayer (to pray for their classmates, family, church, teachers and pastors, and on what they learnt).

CHAPTER ELEVEN

BIRTHRIGHT MATTERS

Session Starter

Let children take turns being blindfolded. In each round one blindfolded child should sit in a chair. The other children can take turns standing in front of the blindfolded person and holding out one hand. The blindfolded person has to guess which person it is by feeling their hand. You could change each round and have the blindfolded person guess an object and guess what it is as well! "In today's story, a blind man tried to recognize his son by feeling his hand."

Genesis 25:27-34, 27:1-45
(Encourage children to open their bibles to the story portion)

The boys grew up and Esau became a skillful hunter, but Jacob was a quiet man staying in his tents. Isaac loved Esau and Rebekah loved Jacob. One day when Jacob was cooking some stew, and Esau returned after hunting was tired so he asked Jacob for some of the red stew. Jacob replied "First sell me your birthright" Esau agreed to it, but Jacob said swear to me first. So, he swore an oath selling his birthright to Jacob in return for stew thereby despising his birthright.

Isaac was old and his eyes were so weak, that he could no longer see. He called for Esau his older son and said to him to get his weapons, go out to the open country to hunt and prepare a kind of tasty food I like and bring it to him that he could eat it and give him his blessing.

Rebekah was listening to Isaac while he said that to Esau and after Esau left, she called out to Jacob and told him what she heard and asked him to bring two choice goats from his flock so she can prepare some tasty food for Isaac just like how he liked it. Jacob said to his mother, but my brother Esau is a hairy man and I am smooth-skinned, what if he touches me and finds out? His mother replied to him let the curse fall on me, just do what I ask you to do. So, he went and brought them to his mom and she prepared it the same way her husband liked.

Rebekah then took some best clothes of Esau and put them over her younger son Isaac. She also covered his hands and the smooth part of his skin with goatskin and handed the food to her son to take to his father. He went to his father and lied saying "I am Esau your firstborn, I have done what you have asked me to do. Please sit up and eat some of the food I have prepared so that you may give me your blessing" Isaac then asked him to come close to him so he can touch and feel him before him his blessing because he felt that the voice was the voice of Jacob and hands felt like the hands of Esau. Then he ate the food and blessed Jacob thinking he was blessing Esau. As soon as Jacob left Isaac, Esau brought food and said " Father, please sit up and eat some food and give me your blessing" Isaac then asked him," Who was it that I just blessed him now?" When he heard that he realized that Jacob had stolen his blessing. He then begged his father to bless him and wept aloud. Esau then held a grudge and wanted to kill him. Rebekah then told him to run away to her brother Laban in Haran as his Esau wanted to kill him. She told him to stay there in Haran and come back only after Esau's anger subsides.

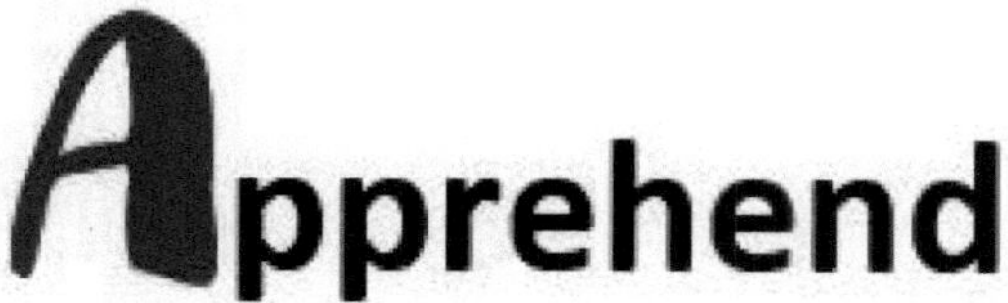

The bible says "he was faint" after his long day in the fields. What do you think of Esau? Do we agree with the decision made by Esau? We have all been in that situation where we had been physically and mentally tired after a long day, and then we want something to help us calm down, and rest - IMMEDIATELY! Sometimes we are like that too right? We don't like to wait for anything! Just like Esau wanted a momentary relief from his discomfort there are a lot of others who trade off hard and good work for a moment of pleasure.

People who take bribes others who choose their own financial gain over others Families choose to divorce after years of love and building a family. Think about what you do? Are you choosing immediate pleasure over spiritual work? What are you looking at? Are you focussing on things that are seen (temporary) or the ones which are unseen (eternal) ?

****

Memory Verse

****

"Genesis 27:28

"May God give you heaven's dew and earth's richness - an abundance of grain and new wine"

"

Blanco

****

****

"Jacob is not a perfect character. Our eyes are not to be fixed on human individuals. We must cast our vision upon God's presence and activity. God is present in the lives of these people. God works redemption, forgiveness, and ultimately, salvation. Such activity may not always be in the forefront of life, but it is

there. Similarly, we can claim, in faith, that God makes redemption available in our lives. As flawed as we might be, or as prone to wrong decisions as Jacob was, we can be confident in God's loving regard, and God's willingness to redeem."

Esau Sells His Birthright

Then Jacob gave Esau some bread and some lentil stew. He ate and drank, and then got up and left. So Esau despised his birthright. Genesis 25:34

The puzzle is based on Genesis 25:19-34

Q	B	T	G	Y	H	B	W	R	N	N	G	O	F	S
P	I	W	O	X	S	I	S	A	A	C	C	T	E	T
K	R	O	W	D	C	O	O	K	I	N	G	W	R	A
F	T	S	N	B	U	A	S	O	J	M	B	I	N	R
W	H	B	K	O	P	S	H	Q	P	Y	L	N	U	V
B	R	N	T	E	J	B	K	P	L	I	H	S	R	I
O	I	V	P	R	O	J	T	K	T	D	S	E	C	N
Y	G	G	E	C	C	D	R	N	A	K	T	T	B	G
S	H	L	A	A	U	X	E	E	H	N	H	D	P	S
K	T	J	S	M	Z	L	R	G	U	N	F	I	Q	C
V	A	E	M	U	Y	B	C	H	B	I	Z	E	M	R
O	C	E	S	A	U	V	T	S	D	A	I	V	J	J
G	H	S	J	K	Q	P	I	F	T	Q	K	O	U	C
S	W	I	L	Y	Q	H	O	M	E	E	U	Z	Z	W
Q	F	E	V	R	E	B	E	K	A	H	W	E	I	T

JACOB	HUNTER	DIE	BREAD	ISAAC
BOYS	HOME	REBEKAH	STEW	ESAU
BIRTHRIGHT	COOKING	TWIN	STARVING	LENTIL

Source: https://www.pinterest.ca/pin/175640454201339150/

Teacher/Student Notes Section

____

____

____

____

Prayer

Ask one of the children in the group if she/he would like to lead the class in prayer (to pray for their classmates, family, church, teachers and pastors, and on what they learnt).

CHAPTER TWELVE

Jacob's New Name

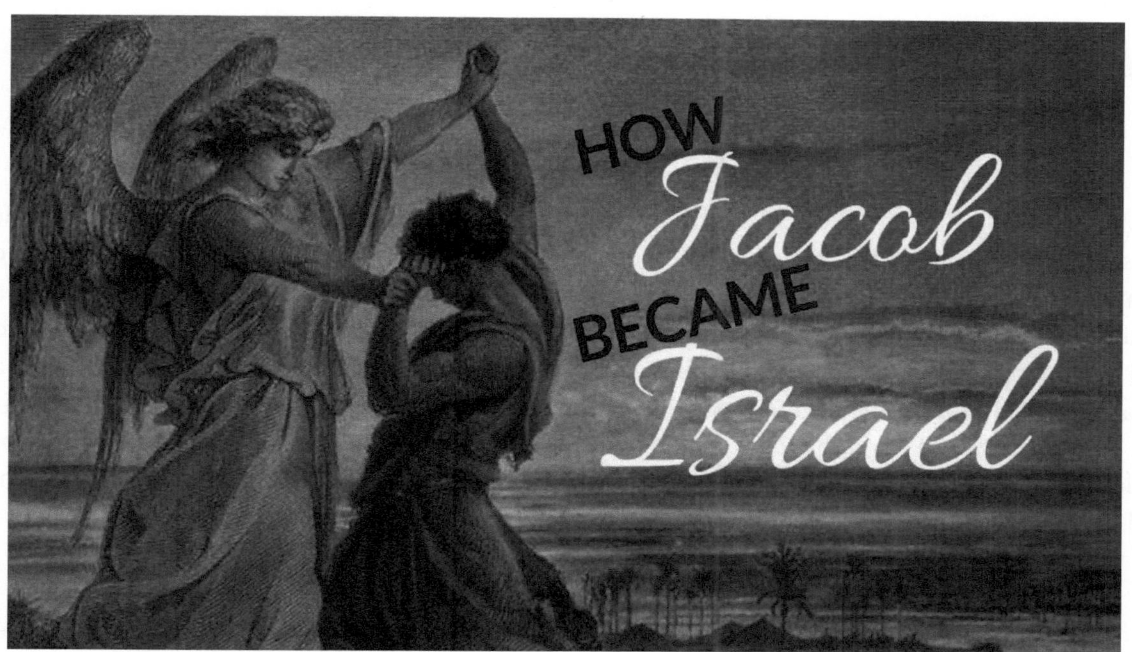

Session Starter

Do you like your name? Do you know what your name means? If given a choice, would you change your name? what would you change your name to? God changed the name of Jacob to Israel. This name meant that God was confirming his covenant to his people.

Genesis 32-33.
(Encourage children to open their bibles to the story portion)

Explain

Jacob sent messengers ahead of him to his brother Esau and he instructed them to say to Esau "Your servant has been staying with Laban. I have cattle, donkeys, sheep goats, male and female servants and am sending this message so that I may find favour in your eyes" The messengers returned to Jacob saying that Esau is coming to meet him with 400 men with him. Jacob was scared, so he divided the people into two groups along with the flocks and herds of animals. Because he thought even if Esau attacks one group, the others may escape.

Then Jacob prayed, "Save me from the hands of my brother Esau, for I am afraid. He had selected a few female and male goats along with camels, donkeys, cows and bulls as a gift for his brother Esau and put them in the care of his servants and asked them to go ahead of him and keep some space between the herds and if Esau were to ask you whom you belong to, tell him that you belong to your servant Jacob and these are your gift sent you my lord Esau and that I will be coming behind. Jacob stayed behind and he took his 2 wives along with 2 female servants and his 11 sons and after he had crossed the ford of Jabok, he sent them all away and was alone and wrestled with a man until daybreak. When the man realized that he could not overpower Jacob, he touched the socket of Jacob's hip. Then the man said let me go for it is daybreak, but he said I will not let you go unless you bless me and he blessed him named him Israel. Jacob named the place Peniel because he saw God face to face and yet his life was spared.

When Jacob saw Esau along with his 400 men, he himself went on ahead and bowed down to the ground seven times as he approached. Esau ran to meet his brother threw his arms around his neck, embraced and kissed him. Then all the female servants and their children, Leah and her children and Rachel and her children all came and bowed down. Esau did not accept any of the gifts and said I already have plenty so keep these for yourself. But Jacob convinced him and then he accepted. Esau wanted to accompany Jacob, but he declined the offer so he went on his way while Jacob went out on his way and settled down.

God had a call on Jacob's life. Though Jacob was running in pursuit of things of life, at God's appointed time Jacob had an encounter with God.

God has a purpose for our life. And through the different situations of our life, God tries to grab our attention towards His call and purpose. One cannot hide from God.

God's plan for our life are beautiful. God's word says in Jeremiah 29:11; The plans I have for you is the plan for a hope and future, plans to prosper and not harm!

Do you see God's plan in your life?

Sometimes we seem to be afraid of God's plan. Discuss why such feeling can creep in to our hearts

Always rememebr - God Loves you!!

****

Memory Verse

****

"Genesis 32:28

And He said, "Your name shall no longer be Jacob, but Israel for you have struggled with God and with men and have prevailed""

****

Christ Connect

****

"God changed his name from Jacob to Israel. That is the reason why Jesus came in to the world that we might have a changed life and to forgive our sins. Jesus' birth, life and resurrection is to show people way to be adopted into God's own family. Just like Jacob, when we are adopted into his family, we will receive a new name- child of God! It does not matter which season or situation of our life we may be in; it is never late. Ask God and receive the spirit of sonship and call him Abba Father."

JACOB WRESTLES WITH GOD

Discover the hidden words.

H	B	L	E	Q	M	I	N	G	N	K	N	C	A	G
I	G	V	W	E	C	J	R	V	X	J	I	Q	E	I
P	A	W	V	T	D	A	I	W	L	I	N	C	I	F
R	W	E	S	A	U	C	M	N	O	E	E	Q	G	T
U	L	T	M	K	O	O	V	E	E	V	W	H	H	S
E	O	A	D	C	V	B	C	R	N	T	Q	T	M	Z
W	R	K	B	Q	G	B	K	W	T	O	V	G	Q	Q
G	B	Q	D	A	X	K	L	H	R	S	N	S	R	N
I	W	P	Z	A	N	V	G	L	N	I	F	W	A	D
T	H	R	E	E	K	I	E	V	E	S	O	L	C	D
P	H	I	G	S	F	G	Y	S	M	N	M	F	H	E
Y	X	S	W	I	I	T	S	B	L	O	I	U	E	G
B	I	Q	H	X	V	E	F	B	L	E	A	H	L	G
T	S	W	G	X	L	P	X	Q	M	V	J	R	A	U
G	O	D	E	B	X	I	S	R	A	E	L	C	Z	H

Word Bank

JACOB	HIP	HUGGED
GIFTS	LABAN	RACHEL
FIGHT	ESAU	LEAH
GOD	ISRAEL	BLESSING

Teacher/Student Notes Section

____

____

____

____

Prayer

Ask one of the children in the group if she/he would like to lead the class in prayer (to pray for their classmates, family, church, teachers and pastors, and on what they learnt).

CHAPTER THIRTEEN

JOSEPH'S DREAMS AND THE IN-BETWEENS

Session Starter

- Do you feel angry at your siblings?
- Will you forgive your brother or sister who fought with you?

- Have any of your friends forgotten about you when you asked them for help?

Genesis 37, 39, and 41.
(Encourage children to open their bibles to the story portion)

Explain

Today we are going to study about Joseph. There was a man named Jacob who lived in Canaan with his family. The land God had promised to his grandfather Abraham and his family. Jacob had 12 sons; however, his favourite son was Joseph. Jacob gave a colourful robe to his favourite son Joseph. Joseph's brothers saw this, and they started hating him more. One day Joseph saw a dream, his dream was "they were trying to gather bunches of grain out in the field when suddenly Joseph's bunch stood up, while all of the rest of the bunches gathered around and bowed to Joseph's bunch of grain." They did not like this and made an angry face at him. The next day he saw another dream that "the sun, moon eleven stars bowing down to him." They became more jealous of him.

Jacob told Joseph to give some food to his brothers. When the brothers saw Joseph coming, they decided to kill him as they were so jealous and angry at their brother Joseph. Reuben did not want to kill Joseph. When Joseph reached, they took his coat and threw him into a nearby pit. Then they saw some People heading to Egypt. They decided to sell Joseph to the travellers as a servant for twenty pieces of silver. The brothers dipped Joseph's colourful robe in the blood of an animal and took it to their father Jacob and said your son Joseph is no more he has been attacked by wild animals. Jacob cried loudly as his favourite son is dead.

Then the travellers who bought Joseph took him to Egypt and sold him to an Egyptian office named Potiphar. God was with Joseph and made him successful at everything he did. Potiphar trusted him in everything and made him in charge of everything in his house. Potiphar's wife tried to get Joseph to sin against God and Potiphar. However, Joseph refused. This made Potiphar's wife angry, so she started telling lies about him to Potiphar and Potiphar believed her and put Joseph in prison. Joseph was blessed even in the prison that, the jail warden put him in charge of the other prisoners. One night, two of the prisoners- Pharaoh's cupbearer and baker both had dreams. The cupbearer dreamed about three branches of the vine. Grapes grew on the vine; the cupbearer squeezed and poured them into the cup of Pharaoh. The baker dreamed that he had three baskets of bread on his head. The top basket had baked goods for Pharaoh, but the birds started eating the baked goods. Joseph told them the meaning of the dream they saw.

Joseph said in three days the cupbearer will continue to serve Pharaoh, whereas the baker will die after three days. Joseph asked the cupbearer to remember him and to tell Pharaoh that he did not deserve to be in jail. The cupbearer did serve Pharaoh again, but he forgot about Joseph.

Two years later, Pharaoh had two dreams. Pharaoh saw seven skinny cows eating seven fat cows, and seven thin heads of grain-eating seven thick heads. No one knew the meaning of this dream. Suddenly the cupbearer remembered about Joseph and told Pharaoh. God told Joseph what Pharaoh's dream meant, and he explained the dreams to Pharaoh. Joseph said, "the dreams represent seven years when plenty of food will grow followed by seven years where no food will grow. You should choose someone to save food during the good years to use it for the bad years." Pharaoh knew God was with Joseph, so he made Joseph second in command in all of Egypt. No one was more powerful than Joseph except for Pharaoh himself. Joseph started to store food during the first seven good years. When the famine came, people from every land came to Egypt to buy grain from Joseph.

What did you learn from this story? What did you find interesting in this story?

Joseph, he remained dependent on God, he never lost his trust even during such power and wealth. He had a vision, and he kept that vision alive, served others wholeheartedly, and remained totally dependent on god. He knew the vision he saw when he was just seventeen years old must be fulfilled. God used this slave boy to save his family and nation. Do you ever have those moments where you ask God, "why me?" I know I do! Somehow, we think we are in full control of our life. When you look at the life of Joseph, even though he had gone through all the trials and temptations; he showed integrity, honest, solid work ethics, his actions showed a confidence in God and he was faithful to God even when it did not feel like God was being faithful to him.

"Do not abandon your God given values in pursuit of your dreams."

—Pete Wilson

****

****

"Ephesians 4:32

Be kind and compassionate to one another, forgiving each other, just as in Christ God forgave you."

****

Christ Connect

****

"Do you recall the story when Jesus healed a man who was unable to walk for thirty-eight years? Some religious leaders were offended that Jesus healed that man on Sabbath. However, the man who was healed realized that he was released from his disease. Similarly, God has a plan for your life. Sometimes, people around you may find it hard to make sense of it; but just like Joseph, be assured that the work of Christ is alive in your life."

Joseph

Old Testament

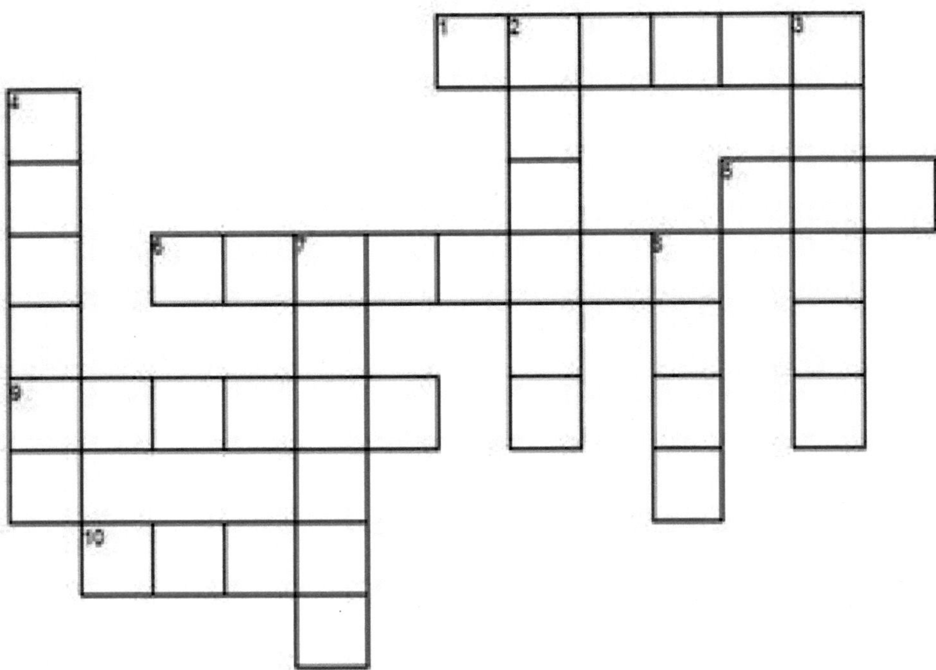

ACROSS

1 God showed Joseph things through _____

5 Joseph interpretted a dream for a baker and told him he would ____

6 Joseph was thrown in prison by ________

9 Joseph had _______ brothers

10 Joseph's father Jacob gave him a ______ of many colors.

DOWN

2 _______ was the mother of Joseph and Benjamin

3 Pharaoh dreamed there were 7 fat cows and 7 ______ cows

4 Joseph told the _______ that his dream meant Pharaoh would restore him to his job

7 Joseph's brothers sold him for ______ pieces of silver

8 Pharaoh gave Joseph his ______ to wear

WORD BANK: Butler, coat, die, dreams, eleven, potiphar, rachel, ring, skinny, twenty.

Source: www.churchhousepuzzles.com

Teacher/Student Notes section

____

____

____

____

Prayer

Ask one of the children in the group if she/he would like to lead the class in prayer (to pray for their classmates, family, church, teachers and pastors, and on what they learnt).

CHAPTER FOURTEEN

JOSEPH'S DREAMS COMES TRUE

Session Starter

- Has there ever been a time when you put your trust in someone and that person failed you? How do you feel about that person? Will you continue to put your trust in them?
- How do you feel when you do something wrong? Does it make you feel bad?
- Is it hard for you to say sorry or to forgive someone who did wrong to you?

Genesis 42, 46, 50.
(Encourage children to open their bibles to the story portion)

Explain

We know that God is all-powerful. He can use sad and hard circumstances for good. Today we will about one-way God turned something meant to harm into something good. How many of you remember the previous lesson? We studied about Joseph and his dream. Does anyone remember the dream Joseph saw? Today we will study how his dream came true. We also saw Pharaoh also had a dream of fat cows and skinny cows, then the skinny cows eating the fat cows. The dream was there will be seven years of plenty of food followed by seven years of famine.

Jacob and his family needed help as they did not have enough food to eat. Nobody had food; food was available only in Egypt. So, Jacob called his 10 sons and told them to go to Egypt to buy food. His last son Benjamin stayed at home. When they reached Egypt, they bowed down before Joseph, the man in charge of the food. The brothers could not recognize Joseph they thought he was a stranger. However, Joseph knew they are his brothers. Many years before they sold him as a servant. Now he had an important job in Egypt and was a very powerful man. The brothers bowed down to Joseph. Joseph's dreams from a long time before were coming true. Joseph decided to test his brothers. "I think you are all spies," Joseph told them. "I know you are here to spy on this land." But the brothers said, "No! we are not spies. We are brothers. We are 12 brothers, but our youngest brother is at home with our father and another brother is dead." Joseph put his brothers in prison for three days. Then he said, bring your youngest brother back to me to prove that you are not spies. But one of you must stay here."

Simeon was put in prison and others went back to Israel with the food for their families. Once they reached their home, they told everything to Jacob what happened, and their father was very upset as he thought he lost his one more son. Later whatever food they have had finished and so Jacob asked his sons to go to Egypt again to get food. First Jacob did not want to send Benjamin with them thinking he might lose him also. As they really needed food, he had no other choice but to send Benjamin along with other brothers. They took money to pay for their food, and they took a special gift for Joseph. Joseph invited all the brothers to his home for a meal.

After the meal, they went on their journey back to Israel. Joseph told his servants to put a silver cup in Benjamin's sack of food. When they reached half away Joseph's, servants came to them asking what you have done by stealing the silver cup of our master. They said whoever has it will be Joseph's slave. When they found out that the silver cup was in Benjamin's sack. They fell to the ground to plead for him as their father Jacob will die without seeing Benjamin. They cannot lose Benjamin!. Joseph could not hold it anymore he told his attendants to go from his house. After they left, he started to cry out aloud and told his brothers," I am Joseph your brother! You sold me to Egypt, but do not be afraid. Godsend me here so I could save your people, a remnant from the famine. Joseph said to his brothers to go home and bring their families back to Egypt, where they would have enough food.

On the way to Egypt, God spoke to Jacob in a vision. A vision like a dream, but Jacob was awake. God said, do not be afraid to go down to Egypt, for I will make you into a great nation there. I will go down with you to Egypt, and I will also bring you back to this land." Jacob's family was blessed in Egypt, But Jacob got older and died. Now Joseph's brothers were afraid that Joseph would punish them for what they did to him. Joseph said," you planned evil against me; God planned it for good, so many people could live." Then Joseph comforted his brothers and spoke kindly to them.

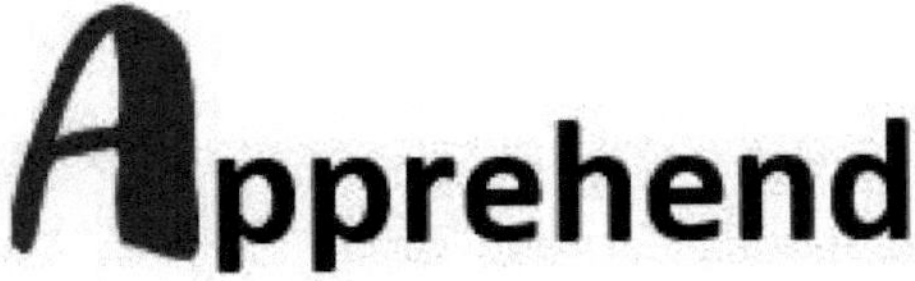

- Can you tell me what happened to Joseph?
  - His brothers sold him into slavery.
- Why did his brothers do this to Joseph?
  - They were jealous of Joseph and the relationship he had with his father.
- How would you feel if you were Joseph?
  - The goal for this question is for us to think whether we would trust our brothers/sisters or someone else for that matter, again. Why? Because Joseph was hurt not just by someone, but by his own brothers! Your family is supposed to love you and support you even when you feel no one else does. If Joseph's own brothers could not love him, then how could he trust anyone else to?
- What emotions would you feel toward God? Do you think it is difficult to put your trust in God Why or why not?
  - Joseph could have been angry at God for putting him in all these situations, but he was not. Instead, he put his trust in God and he knew that when you put your trust in God everything would work out for His glory.

****

Memory Verse

****

"*Genesis 50:19,20*

.. Joseph said to them, "...You intended to harm me, but God intended it for good..."

****

****

"God had a plan for Joseph's life. He allowed Joseph to suffer to rescue a whole nation. In a greater way God planned Jesus to suffer so that many people from all nations would be saved from sins.

Jesus is God the son and the only person who ever lived in this world without sin. He did not deserve to take the punishment, just like Joseph. Jesus took the punishment we deserve and died so that we could have an eternal life with God."

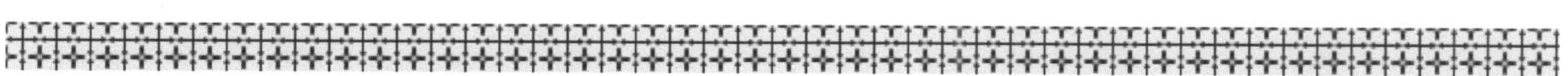

Things required: some stones, plastic bags

Each time you get angry you need to put the rocks in your bag. After some time can you move around with your bag. You might find it difficult because of the weight you have to carry, and you just want to get rid of the burden (rocks). It is the same way when you carry too much hatred with you, you will be weighed down with no energy to do anything. So, we should forgive those who persecute us. Joseph understood that God had a plan for good. He chose to forgive his brothers. Is there someone in your life that you need to forgive? You know that God forgives you, the same way you also chose to forgive others.

God sent Joseph to Egypt to establish a remnant. A remnant is like a remainder, or what is left after something is removed. Many people might have died during the famine, but God saved Jacob and his family through Joseph. Joseph's brothers meant to harm him, but God used it for good to save many people.

In your life when things are good, we tend to shove God to the side. We think that we are in control. However, we come running after him when things go bad in our life. What do you think Joseph did? Joseph trusted God in both times- the good and bad. The same way we should give thanks to Lord in all the times.

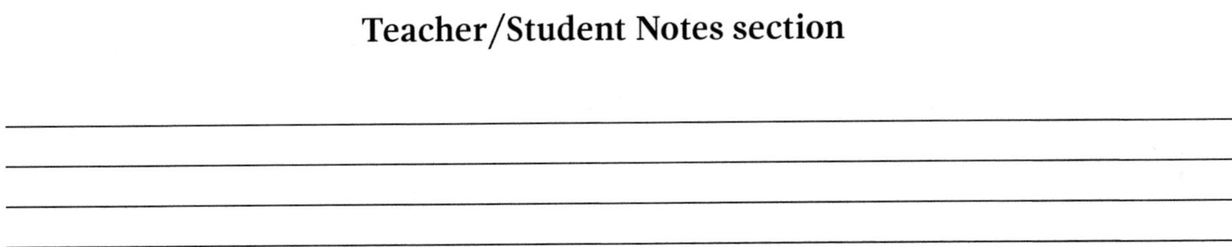

Teacher/Student Notes section

Prayer

Ask one of the children in the group if she/he would like to lead the class in prayer (to pray for their classmates, family, church, teachers and pastors, and on what they learnt).

CHAPTER FIFTEEN

Birth And Call of Moses

Session Starter

What does it feel to lose something or someone we really care for? There is a beautiful story that Jesus tells his disciples a beautiful story of a sheep that was lost and how the shepherd leaves the rest of the sheep and goes searching for the lost sheet. When he finds the sheep, he is happy and he shares the joy with others as well. As we learn the life of Moses, remember, God's plan for every single person is unique and valuable.

Exodus: 1-4
(Encourage children to open their bibles to the story portion)

We learned How God used Joseph's suffering to provide a way for Jacob and his family to survive a famine. As a result, God's people ended up thriving in Egypt.

Joseph brought his family to Egypt. Later Joseph died. His family stayed in Egypt. They were known as Israelites as they came from the family of Jacob, who was called Israel.

A new Pharaoh came to power, and he was afraid of the Israelites. The family had grown so big in number that they might join Egypt's enemies and fight against him. Pharaoh made the Israelites slaves and gave them very hard work to do, but their families kept growing! Pharaoh ordered for all the baby boys to be killed or to throw them in the Nile River.

At this time, a woman gave birth to a son. She tried to hide him for as long as she can. After a while, she couldn't hide him anymore so she made a basket and put him in the basket and set it along the banks of the Nile River. The baby's older sister, Miriam tried to move along with the basket and watched the basket. Soon Pharaoh's daughter went to the river to take a bath. She found the basket; she took it and when opened it. She saw a crying baby. Pharaoh's daughter felt sorry for the baby and wanted him to be her son. The princess named him Moses and she said as I pulled him out of water.

When Moses grew up, he saw an Egyptian man mistreating an Israelite man. Moses killed the Egyptians. Pharaoh found out what Moses did, and He got very angry. So, Moses fled from Egypt. He worked as a shepherd in Midian for many years. Moses got married and had a family. The Israelite people in Egypt were miserable and they cried to God. God heard them, and he planned to help them.

One day, while Moses was watching his sheep, he saw something strange. A bush was on fire, but it was not burning up. From inside the bush, God spoke, "Moses, Moses!" Moses replied, "Here I am." God told Moses to take off his sandals as Moses was standing on the Holy ground. Then God said," I have seen how my people are suffering. I want you to lead them out of Egypt to a new land for them." The new Land is called Canaan. Moses thought if the Israelites even remember that they have a God." What if they ask for Your name? What should I tell them?" "I am Who I am," God said. Tell them: I am has sent me to you." What if they do not believe me? Moses asked. God told Moses to throw his staff on the ground. When he did, the staff became a snake! God told Moses to reach down and grab the snake. It became a staff again! God said, "I will use signs like this to show Pharaoh I have sent you."

Moses still did not believe the Lord. He made his hand diseased and then healed. Moses still made excuses like "I cannot speak properly. Please send someone else. "Now God was angry, but He agreed to send Moses' brother, Aaron, with him. So, Moses returned with Aaron to Egypt. When they arrived, Moses told the Israelites what God had said.

Moses was born into a culture that hated his people. His story is a clear picture of God's sovereignty. Not only Moses' life spared but also Moses's mother was able to take care of him for the Princess. Moses grew up in Pharaoh's house and then spent years shepherding in Midian before god called him for a task. Can you imagine the encounter Moses had with God in the burning bush? God drew a curious Moses to Himself and then spoke:" Moses, Moses!" God identifies Himself as the god of Abraham, of Isaac, and of Jacob. He is giving Moses a task to lead His people out of Egypt. He testified to his own grace." I have observed the misery of my people and I know about their sufferings so I am sending you so that you can lead my people, the Israelites out of Egypt". The most basic and important fact about God is that he exists; He always has and always will exist. God does not change. God revealed to Moses who He is so that the people would trust in Him.

God rescued Moses to deliver His people from captivity. Moses had a greater calling to rescue His children. The same way Jesus had a call to come to earth to save God's people from sin.

- What was the only thing that the people of Israel could do?

____

____

- What do we learn about God here?

____

____

- How does it feel to be heard, remembered seen or known? Share form your experience on these four actions.

____
____
____
____

- Do you think Moses was found by accident, or was it God's plan?

____
____
____
____

- How do we see God's protection in this story?

____
____

****

Memory Verse

****

"Exodus 3:12
And God said, "I will be with you. And this will be the sign to you that it is I who have sent you: When you have brought the people out of Egypt, you will worship God on this mountain.""

****

Christ Connect

****

"God saved Moses' life when the king announced to kill all the baby boys under two years old, the same way Jesus was saved when King Herod declared to kill all the boys less than two years. God called Moses to rescue the Israelites from slavery. The calling of Moses points to a greater calling and rescue, the call of Jesus is to come to earth to save God's people. Jesus gave up His life to save u from slavery to sin. Moses first refused to do God's work and made excuses, whereas Jesus willingly obeyed God's plans."

Moses and the Burning Bush

"Do not come any closer," God said. "Take off your sandals, for the place where you are standing is holy ground." Exodus 3:5 (NIV)

The puzzle is based on Exodus 3:1-15

X M V H O I W S G U U Y O I J
P P H M P U P H A R K E I L H
P G Q H H C X L W N O Q Q O O
I F U O B N P S F R D U T O L
Z R I N U G L I L U Y A N K Y
A L U E R C L G O Y N O L D D
R F B Y N F B H C E W R E S U
J G O D R K A T K P Z U B Y F
R V L H L S F B F M L I G O V
C B D I W W N U B Q O N A P E
E Z M J K I L S O E I S D F H
V I B E C Y B H X W C N E U N
S B S M Z B L G O B A E Q S K
J A D D X S L L K L U W M Z H
Y R E T W E F S T R A N G E A

LAND	MILK	STRANGE	FLOWING	SANDALS
FLOCK	LOOK	HOLY	BUSH	HONEY
GOD	MOSES	GROUND	BURN	SIGHT

Source: https://sermons4kids.com/moses_and_the_burning_bush_wordsearch.htm

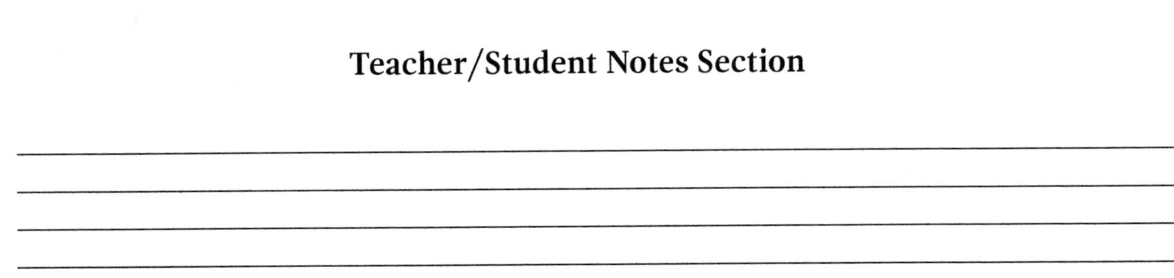

Teacher/Student Notes Section

Prayer

Ask one of the children in the group if she/he would like to lead the class in prayer (to pray for their classmates, family, church, teachers and pastors, and on what they learnt).

CHAPTER SIXTEEN

THE GREAT SIGNS AND WONDERS

Session Starter

Discuss miracles with the children. What is a miracle? Have you ever seen a miracle? What is your favorite miracle from the Bible? You can also have some of the children look up the word miracle in a regular dictionary and in a Bible dictionary.

Exodus 5–14
(Encourage children to open their bibles to the story portion)

Explain

God's people, the Israelites, were slaves in Egypt. They cried out to God, and God called Moses to rescue them. Moses and his brother Aaron went to Pharaoh: "This is what the Lord, the God of Israel, says: Let My people go." However, Pharaoh replied," who is this Lord? Why should I obey Him? I will not let your people go." So God sent ten plagues to punish the Egyptians. First, God turned the water in the Nile River into the blood. But Pharaoh would not let the people go. God sent frogs into Egypt. Pharaoh said, "Ask your God to take away the frog then I will let you people go." But when God removed the frogs, Pharaoh refused to let the people go. So God sent gnats into Egypt that bit the people and animals. Then God sent flies, and He caused all the livestock to die. Still, Pharaoh did not let the people go. God sent boils that covered the people in Egypt, But Pharaoh's heart was hard. Not even a terrible hailstorm changed Pharaoh's mind. Locust ate up the plants, and then the darkness covered the land for three days. But still, Pharaoh said no to them.

God told Moses, "I will bring one more plague after that, Pharaoh will let you go." Moses warned Pharaoh, God will go through Egypt, and every firstborn male in the land of Egypt will die. There will be a great cry in Egypt, but none of the Israelites will be harmed. Then you and your officials will come down and will tell us to leave." Despite Moses' warning, Pharaoh did not let the Israelites go. God gave the Israelites specific instructions to prepare for that night. Every Israelite family would kill a lamb or a goat and sprinkle its blood on the doorposts of their houses. This would be a special mark that God would see and "pass over" the houses of the Israelites. No one in their families would die. God also told them to eat the lamb as a meal at midnight. The lamb was to be unblemished: no broken bones, no marks, no deformities. They were also to eat unleavened bread (bread without yeast) and bitter herbs. God said, "When you eat it, get dressed and put on your sandals. Eat the meal quickly and be ready to go." The Israel families obeyed God's instructions and got everything ready. While the Egyptians were sleeping, the Israelites were busy making a meal and putting blood on their doorposts.

Then at midnight, God struck every firstborn in the land of Egypt. Pharaoh's son died. The prisoner's son died. The firstborn of the livestock died. There was a great cry in the land of Egypt because there was not a single house without someone dead, Pharaoh called for Moses and Aaron and said," Getup leave my people and go worship Yahweh as you have asked." The Israelites were ready! A whole army of them-600,000 men and their families -left Egypt quickly. They took with them bread and their animals. The Israelites even asked the Egyptians for their riches like gold and silver, and the Egyptians were so afraid that they handed them over! God led his people out of Egypt. He was preparing a place for them in a land called Canaan for 430 years; the Israelites had been slaves in the land of Egypt. They were finally free.

Moses always knew which direction to go because God put a tall pillar of cloud in front of them to point the way. At night they followed a tall pillar of fire. They never got lost because God was with them in guiding the path. Eventually, the pillar stopped by the water called the Red Sea. Meanwhile back in Egypt the Pharaoh and his officials began thinking about the Israelites leaving Egypt. They started to have a second thought about who will do their work if they leave Egypt. So Pharaoh decided to chase after Israelites and make them come back. He sent all of his horses and chariots and all of his horsemen and troops.

When God's people saw the Egyptian army approaching in the distance they became very afraid. There was nowhere to getaway. The army was behind and the red sea was in front of them. The people complained to their leader, Moses. They said," Why did you lead us out of Egypt into the desert to die? We would have been better off to have stayed in Egypt."

But Moses said," Do not be afraid. Stand firm and you will see how God will save you today. The Egyptian can never win because God will fight for you." An angel of God had been travelling in front of the Israelites and he moved back behind them along with the pillar of cloud. The cloud blocked the view of the Egyptians and they could only see night and darkness. At God's command Moses stretched out his big staff (stick) over the water and it began to change. A strong wind blew the water up into two walls of water on each side and dry land down the middle. God had provided a way to cross the sea to the other side. When the Egyptians saw the dry land they followed the Israelites. Now that the Israelites were all safely on the other side God told Moses to stretch his staff over the water again. Soon all of the Egyptian armies were drowned in the water. The people were so happy that God had saved them from their enemies. Moses wrote a song about what happened and everyone sang it. And Moses' sister Miriam sang another part of the song. Then she got a tambourine and began to dance. Soon all of them were dancing with joy for all God had done that day.

What an amazing story of God's faithfulness and power! You know, during a few of the plagues, Pharaoh's magicians were able to mimic the things God did. That might have lead Pharaoh to continue thinking that the false gods he worshiped were also powerful. But the funny thing is that when God had sent a plague, mimicking the plague wouldn't help anything.

When God filled the land with frogs, making more frogs did not help at all. The false Egyptian gods were actually powerless! They could not undo God's plans. God sent the plagues to judge the Egyptians for worshiping false gods. Egypt had a false god of the river, but God turned the river to blood. They had a false god of medicine, but God make them sick with boils and sores. They had a false god of the sun, but God covered the land in darkness. No matter which false god the Egyptians might have prayed to, the one true God was proving that only He has power. Finally, God sent the last plague, the death of the firstborn sons. In a way, it mirrored what Pharaoh had tried to do to the people of Israel by killing all their sons.

God gave the Israelites special instructions on how to avoid the final plague. God's people were to kill a spotless lamb and spread its blood over their doorposts. That would serve as a sign, and the firstborn sons would be protected in those homes. In addition, the people were to eat the meat of the lamb that night, with bread that they could make quickly. You guessed it, unleavened bread—like matzo! God wanted them to be dressed, with their sandals on their feet, ready to leave Egypt as soon as the plague was over. God delivered His people and proved that He is the one true God.

****

Memory Verse

****

"Exodus 13:14
In days to come, when your son asks you, 'What does this mean?' say to him, 'With a mighty hand the Lord brought us out of Egypt, out of the land of slavery."

****

Christ Connect

****

"The final plague did more than prove God's power to Egypt, it pointed forward to when Jesus would come. By His grace, God spared the Israelites from judgment by requiring the blood of a lamb. Jesus is the Lamb of God, who takes away the sin of the world. His death was the ultimate sacrifice, and those who trust in Christ are under His saving blood and will be passed over in the final judgment."

Do

Let children remember how God delivered his people from Pharoah, as they do the crossword sheet.

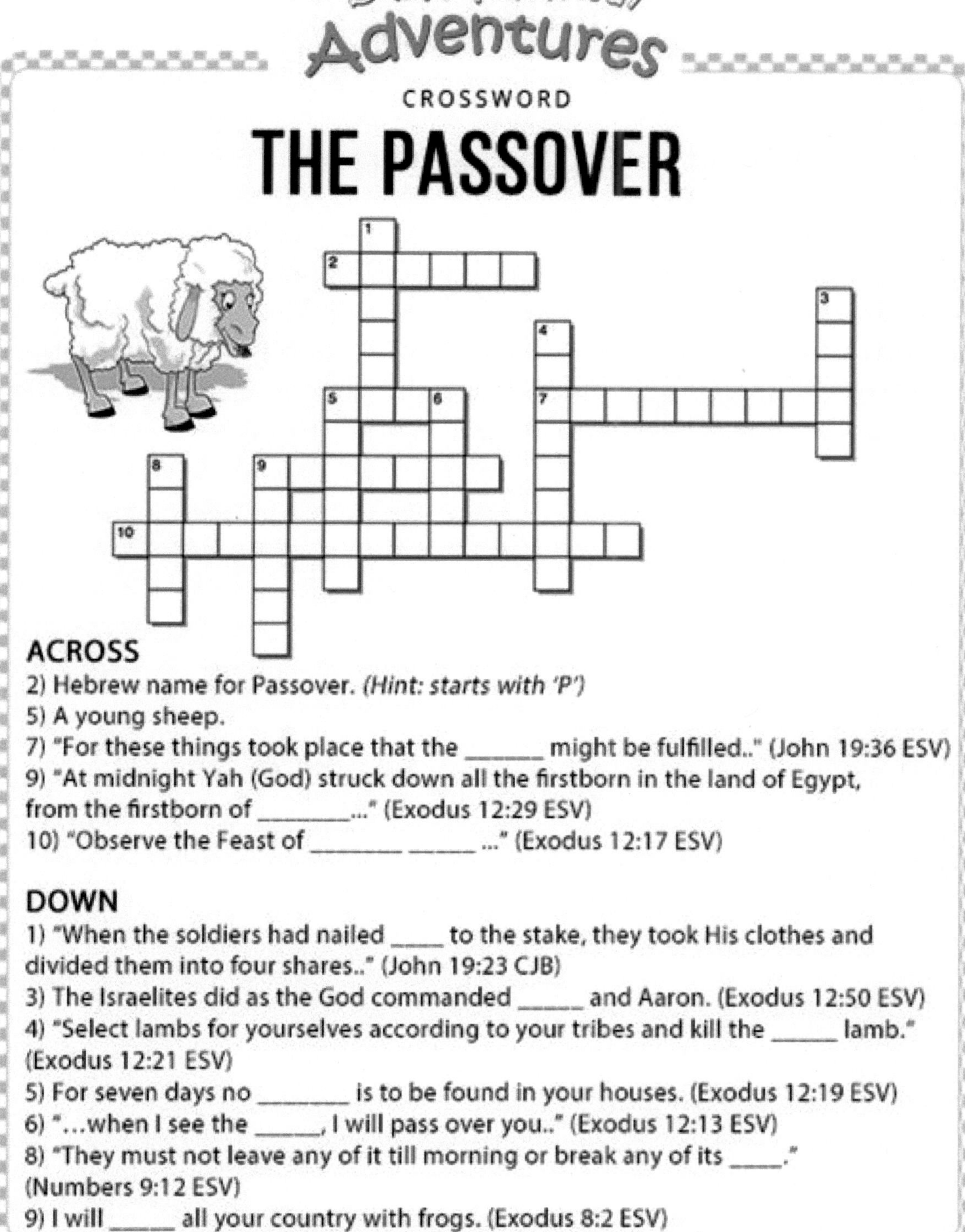

Bible Pathway Adventures

CROSSWORD

THE PASSOVER

ACROSS

2) Hebrew name for Passover. *(Hint: starts with 'P')*
5) A young sheep.
7) "For these things took place that the ______ might be fulfilled.." (John 19:36 ESV)
9) "At midnight Yah (God) struck down all the firstborn in the land of Egypt, from the firstborn of ________..." (Exodus 12:29 ESV)
10) "Observe the Feast of ________ ______..." (Exodus 12:17 ESV)

DOWN

1) "When the soldiers had nailed ____ to the stake, they took His clothes and divided them into four shares.." (John 19:23 CJB)
3) The Israelites did as the God commanded _____ and Aaron. (Exodus 12:50 ESV)
4) "Select lambs for yourselves according to your tribes and kill the ______ lamb." (Exodus 12:21 ESV)
5) For seven days no ________ is to be found in your houses. (Exodus 12:19 ESV)
6) "...when I see the ______, I will pass over you.." (Exodus 12:13 ESV)
8) "They must not leave any of it till morning or break any of its _____." (Numbers 9:12 ESV)
9) I will _____ all your country with frogs. (Exodus 8:2 ESV)

For free Bible resources and Teacher Packs including coloring pages, worksheets, quizzes and more visit our website at: biblepathwayadventures.com

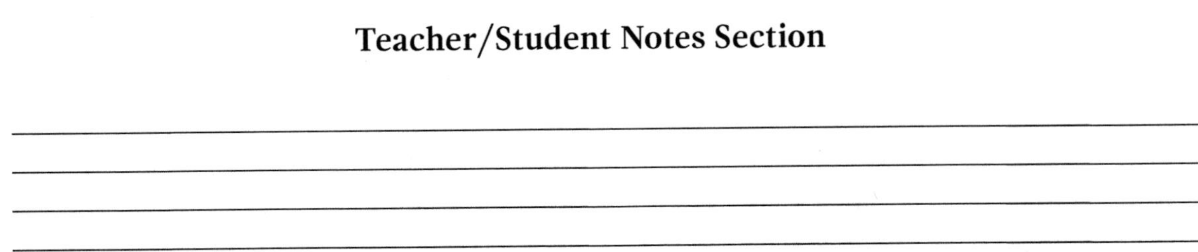

Teacher/Student Notes Section

Prayer

Ask one of the children in the group if she/he would like to lead the class in prayer (to pray for their classmates, family, church, teachers and pastors, and on what they learnt).

CHAPTER SEVENTEEN

THE SEVERE TEST

Session Starter

The game we will play is called "What is it?"

Place items in brown paper bags, such as breadcrumbs, interlocking bricks, marbles, or other small objects. Let the kids take turns reaching into the bag to feel the items. Allow each kid to whisper a guess in your ear. Tell him if he is correct, but remind kids not to share the answer with anyone until every kid has had a chance to feel the item.

Exodus 15:22–17:7
(Encourage children to open their bibles to the story portion)

Explain

In today's lesson, we're learning about a cool story of how God provided for his people, the Israelites. Remember, God used Moses to rescue his people from slavery in Egypt and He led them toward the Promised Land. But, the journey was long and the people got grumpy. Moses led God's people away from the Red Sea, and they came to the wilderness. They could not find good water to drink, and they complained to Moses. God said, "If you obey Me and do what is right and keep My commands, I will not punish you like I punished the Egyptians. I am the LORD who heals you."

The Israelites came to a place called Elim, where they found plenty of food and water. They camped there. The Israelites left Elim and journeyed into the wilderness. They were hungry. They complained to Moses. "We wish we had died in Egypt! At least there was food to eat," they said. "You brought us out here to starve to death!" But Moses had not brought them out there to die. God knew what He was doing. God said, "I have heard the complaints of the Israelites. Tell them: In the evening you will eat meat, and in the morning you will eat bread until you are full. Then you will know that I am the Lord your God."

So in the evening, quail came into the camp. In the morning, fine flakes like frost were on the ground. "What is it?" the Israelites asked. Moses said, "It is the bread the LORD has given you to eat." The Israelites called the bread manna, which means "what is it?" God gave the people instructions. He told them to collect just enough to eat for the day. If they collected too much, the leftovers went bad. He told them to collect twice as much on the sixth day because the seventh day was the Sabbath, a day to rest. The Israelites did not always follow God's instructions. Sometimes they collected too much manna, and sometimes they tried to collect manna on the Sabbath day. Moses was angry that the people refused to obey God. The Israelites ate manna for 40 years while they were in the wilderness.

The Israelites moved about the wilderness as the Lord told them to do. One day, they came to a camp with no water. "Give us something to drink," they told Moses. "Why are you complaining to me?" Moses asked. "You brought us out here to die," the Israelites said. They forgot that the Lord had a plan for them. "Lord, what should I do?" Moses cried out. God showed Moses a rock and instructed him to hit it with his staff. Water came out of it, and the people drank. It was a sign that the Lord was with them.

What a story! Can you relate to this story? Do you complain when you are hungry? Do you get angry when you are super hungry? But here is the thing: Complaining never solves anything. It reveals that we are ungrateful, and our focus is much on what we don't have as opposed to what God has given us. And complaining against God, the one true God who showed His power and glory in the most incredible ways to rescue the Israelites from slavery: Well, that is sinful and just plain foolishness! Thankfully, no matter how sinful or foolishly people behave, God still loves us. Instead of punishing the Israelites, God provided them for the physical need of His people.

Moses struck a rock and water poured out. Quail came into the camp for the people to catch and cook. And in the morning, flaky bread covered the ground. God's provision was so miraculous, the people did not know what was it at first; they even called it Manna, which means "What is it?" God had rules for manna. He told them to collect only as much as they needed for the day. Each family was to collect one day's worth of manna. If they collected extra that would go bad. God was basically forcing the, to rely on Him each day, it was tough God were asking them, "Do you trust me?" Will you trust me tomorrow? Each day, God taught them how to trust Him a little more. So, what we need to do, we need to trust him no matter what situation we are.

Think about the following:

- What is something you've complained about in the last week?
  Does complaining ever really get us anywhere?

  ____
  ____

- Why was it wrong for the people to complain about their hunger in the wilderness?

  ____
  ____

- Why do you think God only allowed them to collect enough manna for one day?

  ____
  ____

- What are some ways we distrust God today? How can we trust Him more each day?

  ____
  ____

- How does this story remind us of God's goodness?

  ____
  ____

****

Memory Verse

****

"Exodus 15:11
Who among the gods is like you, Lord? Who is like you? Majestic in holiness, awesome in glory, working wonders?"

****

****

"In this story, when difficult situations occurred, the people of Israel could ask the Lord. Instead, they murmured and even tried to argue with their leader, Moses. God brought the Israelites out of Egypt and had a perfect plan for them. However, they kept forgetting that when times were difficult. Jesus asked the blind man, "What do you want me to do for you?" And the blind man said, "My Lord, I want to see". Remember that Jesus is not away from us in times of need.

Jesus came for the blind man just beside him. He is never far away; especially when you are in need. All you need to do is to recognize that He will answer you if you call out to Him. Jesus said, "If you ask anything in My Name, I will do it (John 14:14). That is His promise. He knows our needs and dreams and ambitions. You need to commit them to God and let Him lead the way."

Dinner on the Ground

"I have heard the grumbling of the Israelites. Tell them, 'At twilight you will eat meat, and in the morning you will be filled with bread. Then you will know that I am the LORD your God.' "
Exodus 16:12 (NIV)

```
N P C C R T Q U A I L H T C H
U T H B A N D A C A M P I P E
F D S E S O B D M E I T C B A
B M M O O W R D E O G A V E V
T S C F V R E H U A R Y R A E
Y W S K E I A A Z O T N P T N
D Q I H Z D D D A A T H I T L
S F T L D E S E R T N M O N D
T A J S I X W E Y O M O K F G
G H G D P G V E R G H S G I T
C Z R W C R H A P K E E W H I
P O W P A S A T Q N U S G C A
L Q S T X R G R U M B L E D Y
E P S I S W V E N O U G H E A
V I Q I S R A E L I T E S Y H
```

desert	Israelites	starve	gather	twilight
grumbled	Egypt	death	enough	quail
Moses	meat	LORD	bread	camp
Aaron	food	heaven	morning	eat

Source: https://sermons4kids.com/manna_wordsearch.htm

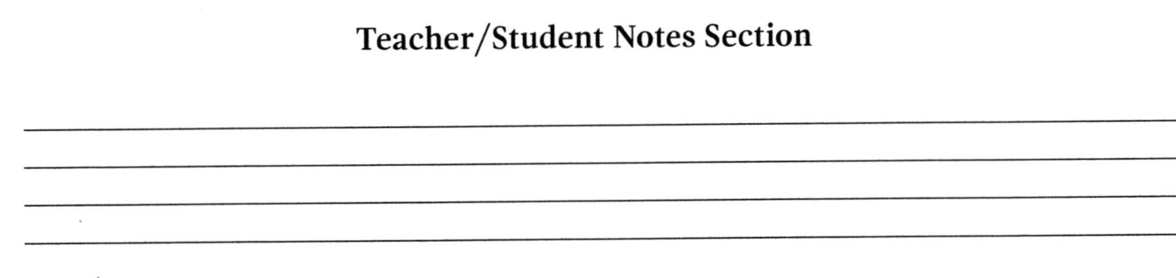

Teacher/Student Notes Section

Prayer

Ask one of the children in the group if she/he would like to lead the class in prayer (to pray for their classmates, family, church, teachers and pastors, and on what they learnt).

CHAPTER EIGHTEEN

THE GOLDEN CALF

Session Starter

We are just going to discuss a few scenarios.

Can you think of your most favorite sportsperson or the coolest person you have ever come across? Why is that person so special to you? What is the longest time you can sit away from not looking at your mobile phone? Why do you think you feel that way? Today, we are going to discuss a very special story on understanding what/who must occupy the most important place of our life.

Exodus 32:1-35; 34:1-9
(Encourage children to open their bibles to the story portion)

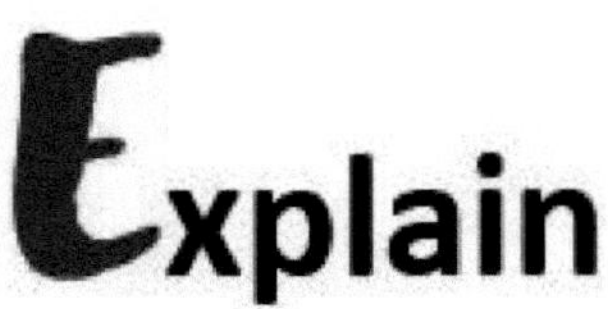

God had delivered the Israelites from slavery in Egypt and Pharaoh. The Israelites came to Mount Sinai, and they camped there in front of the mountain. Moses went up the mountain, and God spoke to him. God had a lot to tell Moses, and he was up on Mount Sinai for 40 days and 40 nights. Meanwhile, the Israelites at the bottom of the mountain were getting impatient. They began to wonder, where Moses is. What is taking him so long? Is he still alive? One day they said to Aaron, "we know something dreadful has happened to Moses because he does not come back." Of course, they complained because Moses had led them into the lonely wilderness and left them without a brave leader to take his place. Every day they grew more restless.

Finally, they told Aaron, "Make us gods to go before us and show us the way." Aaron was not brave. He feared the people. He remembered the time when they wanted to kill Moses because they could find no water. Perhaps he thought they would kill him if he refused to do as they asked. He did not remind them of their promise to serve no gods but God. Instead, he told them, bring your gold earrings to means and the people did. Aaron melted the gold carefully in the fire. Then he shaped the gold into the form of a calf like the ones the Egyptians worshiped. And the people said to one another," These are the Gods, O Israel, that brought you up out of Egypt." This is the golden calf that they could worship.

God saw what the people were doing, and he was very angry because of their sin. God told Moses to go down the mountain. "I will destroy those people," God said. Moses said, "God please forgive them". "Remember all the promises you have made with Abraham, Isaac and Jacob. You promised to give them as many offspring as there are stars in the sky. You promised to bless them and give them land." So God decided not to destroy the people. Moses went down the mountain. He carried two stone tablets on which God had written the laws. Moses got closer to camp and saw that people were dancing before the golden calf. He threw down the stone tablets, smashing them at the bottom of the mountain. Then he destroyed the calf they made. "What were you thinking?" Moses asked Aaron. The people were out of control.

The next day, Moses went back up the mountain to talk to God. These people have sinned against you," Moses said, "please forgive their sin." God told Moses to return to people." When the time comes, I will punish them for their sin."Then the Lord sent a plague a terrible sickness to the people because they worshipped the golden calf. God continued to meet with Moses and give him law and instructions. He made two more stone tablets to replace the ones Moses broke. One morning, Moses went up the mountain to meet with God. The Lord came down in a cloud. He said," The Lord is a compassionate and gracious God. But he will not leave the guilty unpunished." Moses bowed down and worshipped God. Lord, please go with us," he said. "Forgive our sin and accept us as your people."

Here is a story in the Bible about people who were supposed to love God––but do you know what they really loved. They really loved gold––so they made a Golden Calf out of their gold––and they began to worship the Golden Calf instead of God.

How do you suppose it made God feel to see those people loving that Golden Calf instead of loving God? (Give the children a chance to answer.) It made God feel really bad, because God had taken care of those people. They had been slaves in Egypt, and God helped them to escape. They had run short of water, but God gave them plenty of water to drink. They had run short of food, so God fed them. They had plenty of reasons to love God–but they really loved their Golden Calf.

When God saw them dancing around their Golden Calf, he punished them. They had to grind up their Golden Calf into a fine powder––and mix it with water––and drink it. They didn't love that! I don't know what gold tastes like, but I don't ever want to have to grind up any gold into a powder and then drink it! How about you! God punished them for the same reason that your parents sometimes punish you. God wanted them to remember not to do something like that again. God wanted to remind them that he was the one they should love––not some old Golden Calf.

And it worked! Those people made other mistakes, but they never again made themselves a Golden Calf. Whenever they thought about what they had done, it reminded them to love God instead of gold. They did something else really good too. They told their children and their grandchildren what they had done, so their children and grandchildren would never make the kind of mistake they had made. They wanted their children and grandchildren to love God instead of gold.

Sometimes we are tempted to love things that aren't really very important. You might love your toys. That's OK as long as your toys don't become more important to you than God. Jesus said that we should love God more than anything else––and he said that if we did that, God would give us the other things that we need (Matthew 6:33).

God loves you and takes care of you. Don't forget to love God.
Discuss within the group the following questions:

- In this story, what did God want the people to stop doing?
- What do you think the people should have been doing?

Memory Verse

"*Exodus 34:5, 6*

And the Lord came down... and He passed in front of Moses, proclaiming, "The Lord, the Lord, the compassionate and gracious God, slow to anger, abounding in love and faithfulness"

Christ Connect

"***God's people sinned against God, and Moses asked God to forgive them. Moses acted as their mediator, standing for them before God. Moses could not do anything to make up for their sin, but we have a better Mediator—Jesus. Jesus paid for our sin on the cross and stands for us before God. When we trust in Jesus, our sins are forgiven.***"

CROSSWORD

THE GOLDEN CALF

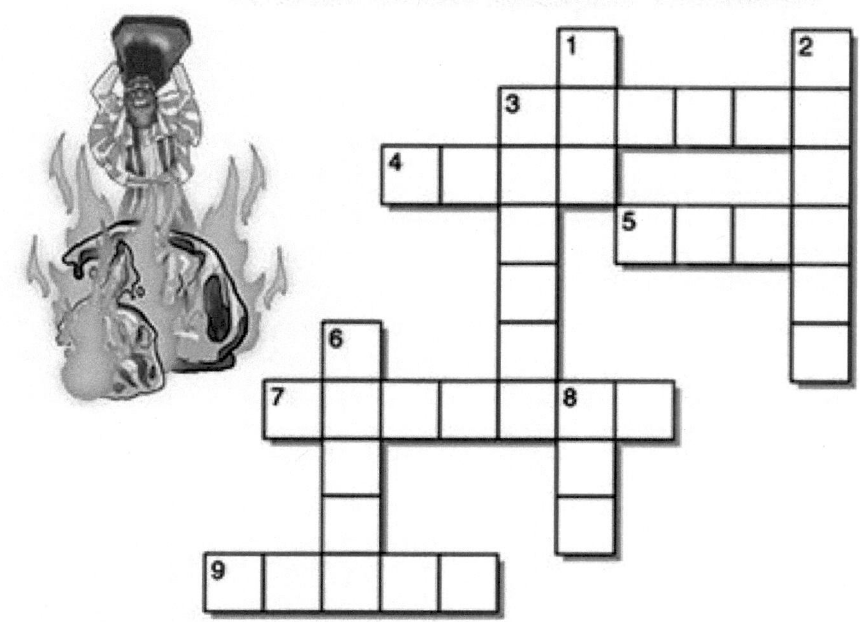

ACROSS

3) Moses made the Israelites drink this. (Exodus 32:20 ESV)
4) Aaron used this metal to make a calf. (Exodus 32:4 ESV)
5) Moses burned the calf in the _______ . (Exodus 32:20 ESV)
7) Moses threw these on the ground and broke them. (Exodus 32:19 ESV)
9) Now Mount ______ was wrapped in smoke because Yah (God) had descended on it in fire. (Exodus 19:11 ESV)

DOWN

1) "And _____ spoke all these words..." (Exodus 20:1 ESV)
2) Aaron was the first High _______. (Exodus 28:1-5 ESV)
3) God sent a plague on the people, because they made the calf..." (Exodus 32:35 ESV)
6) People took off their gold rings and gave them to _____. (Exodus 32:3 ESV)
8) Moses carried _______ stone tablets down the mountain. (Exodus 32:15 ESV)

Source: https://biblepathwayadventures.com/activities/golden-calf-2/

Teacher/Student Notes Section

____

____

____

____

Prayer

Ask one of the children in the group if she/he would like to lead the class in prayer (to pray for their classmates, family, church, teachers and pastors, and on what they learnt).

CHAPTER NINETEEN

THE 10 COMMANDMENTS - LOVE GOD

Session Starter

Draw a line using a chalk or place cones to create a border, give the children an inflated balloon and tell the kids to keep the balloon up in the air without stepping out of the border for 2 mins. The Israelites were given a different boundary line to keep.

Exodus 19:1-20:11; 31:18
(Encourage children to open their bibles to the story portion)

Three months after the Israelites left Egypt they came to the desert of Sinai and camped in front of the mountain.

The Lord called Moses from the mountain and said This is what you should tell the Israelites "You have seen what I did to the Egyptians and how I had rescued him". If you listen carefully to me and keep my covenant, you will be my people. And God made a covenant with his people that day.
Moses went back to the people and told them what the Lord had said and they agreed to what the Lord had said. The Lord said to Moses, I am going to come to you in a dense cloud so that the people will hear me speaking with you and will always put their trust in you. The Lord asked Moses to inform people to consecrate themselves today and that the people came out of the camp to meet the Lord and they stood close to the foot of the mountain.

God came down the mountain, smoke covered the mountain, the mountain shook and the trumpet sounded louder when God came down and gave Moses the Ten Commandments written on 2 stone tablets which had the commandments engraved by the Lord of God.

Why do you think God gave us rules? Why is it important to obey the rules God gave us? ***Why did God give Moses 10 commandments?*** God gave rules as to how we should love Him and others. God is holy and he wants his people to be holy like him. There was a physical manifestation of God's presence on the mountain. Thunder, lightning and cloud signalled God's presence. The people of Israel heard the trumpet sound and they trembled. The people also came out of their camp to meet up with God where they could see, smell, see and feel the presence of God, but they couldn't go any further closer to the mountain. ***How do you react when you cannot cross boundaries God or your parents made for you? Is it easy or difficult? Do you feel tempted to cross the boundaries once in a while?***

The first 5 commandments teach us in great detail about our relationship between us and God that will help us understand who God is and what he expects from us. Tells us that we should love the Lord our God with all heart, with all our soul, with all our mind and all our strength. It is the most important commandment- Love the Lord. ***How easy or difficult is it to obey this commandment?***

****

Memory Verse

****

"Exodus 20:5, 6 (MSG)
I am God, your God, ... loyal to the thousands who love me and keep my commandments."

****

Christ Connect

****

"God made a covenant with his people. In Exodus 19:5-6 God says " If you obey me, you will be my people" But the people did not obey God, instead they disobeyed a lot of times. But every time they disobeyed, Moses stood up for the people and acted as their advocate. We might not have Moses in our lives, but we do have Jesus who acts as a mediator for us with God. How often do you turn to Jesus?"

Do

The Ten Commandments

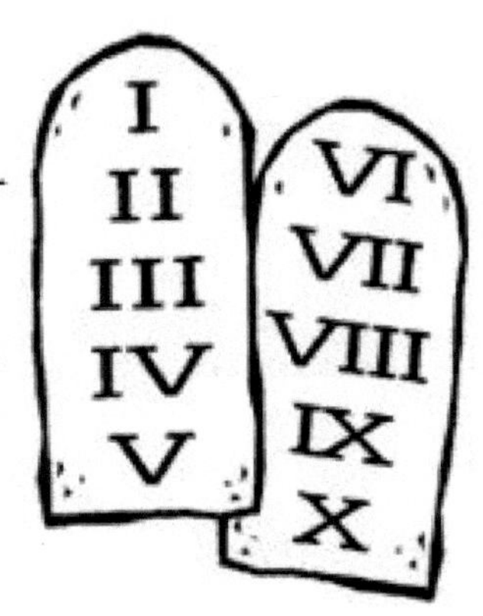

And God spoke all these words: "I am the LORD your God, who brought you out of Egypt, out of the land of slavery. "You shall have no other gods before me." Exodus 20:1-3

Based on Exodus 20:1-17 (NIV)

ACROSS

2. You shall not make for yourself an ______. (a false god)
5. You shall have no other _______ before me.
7. You shall ______ commit adultery.
8. You shall not _______. (kill)
9. You shall not give ______ testimony against your neighbor. (untrue)

DOWN

1. You shall not _______. (to want something that belongs to another)
3. ________ your father and your mother.
4. Remember the Sabbath day by keeping it ______.
6. You shall not ______. (to take what does not belong to you)
7. You shall not misuse the ______ of the LORD your God.

FALSE	IDOL	STEAL	HONOR	MURDER
NAME	COVET	HOLY	NOT	GODS

Source: https://sermons4kids.com/ten_commandments_crossword.htm

Teacher/Student Notes Section

____

____

____

____

Prayer

Ask one of the children in the group if she/he would like to lead the class in prayer (to pray for their classmates, family, church, teachers and pastors, and on what they learnt).

CHAPTER TWENTY

THE 10 COMMANDMENTS - LOVE OTHERS

Session Starter

Fix 4 spots in a room, name them I love it, hate it, okay, like it. Now name different things and ask the kids to go to the appropriate spots depending on their preferences.

Exodus 20:12-17
(Encourage children to open their bibles to the story portion)

It had been about three months since the Israelites had been rescued from slavery in Egypt. The Israelites along with Moses were camped near Mt. Sinai. God told the Israelites "If you listen carefully to me and keep my covenant, you will be My people" and the Israelites agreed to do everything the Lord said. Moses went up the mountain and the Lord came down in fire and there was smoke covering the mountain. There was thunder, lightning, the mountain shook and a loud trumpet sounded. God told them not to come up the mountain.

Then God gave Moses the ten commandments. The first four commandments talk about loving God and the last six commandments told the Israelites how to have a good relationship with one another. You must honour your father and mother. You must not murder. You must keep your marriage pure; you must not steal, not lie and must not take away what belongs to another person. Moses was on the mountain for 40 days. After God finished speaking to Moses on Mt. Sinai, he gave Moses two stone tablets that he had written with his own finger.

The ten commandments teach us not only how to love the Lord but also love others. It starts with honouring our parents, its okay to disagree with them, but the scripture tells us to honour our parents. It also focusses on valuing others by forgiving them. Also says that staying committed in a relationship and that it is wrong to take and use something without the knowledge of the person that belongs to and that it is wrong to lie and to want something that doesn't belong to you. ***Which one from the above is the most difficult for you to follow and why? How difficult is it to love your enemies?***

Do you know that Bible asks you to bless those who curse you? ***Is it an easy or difficult thing for you to love those who hate you?***

****

Memory Verse

****

"*Exodus 20:12*

Honour your father and mother, so that you may live long in the land the Lord your God is giving you"

****

****

"God gave us laws to show what he wants us to do and how he wants us to be. There is not one person in the whole wide world who is righteous. The scripture says, all have sinned and fallen short of the glory of God. And God doesn't want us to perish, that's why he sent us his only son Jesus to take away the punishment we deserve.

When we love God, we would obey his commandments. All we have to do is to try to obey, yes, we would fall and fail multiple times but remember that we have a God who will help us, forgive our sins and help us inherit eternal life."

Do

Ask the kids to write a letter to the parents either asking for forgiveness or thanking them for everything that they have done for them

Teacher/Student Notes Section

____

____

____

____

Prayer

Ask one of the children in the group if she/he would like to lead the class in prayer (to pray for their classmates, family, church, teachers and pastors, and on what they learnt).

CHAPTER TWENTY-ONE

THE TABERNACLE

Session Starter

Give children a bunch of disposable cups and ask them to make a tower (without the kids able to see what the other ones are making). Is it easy to make the tower with or without instructions? Compare the different towers made by the kids and discuss.

Exodus 35:4-40:38
(Encourage children to open their bibles to the story portion)

When God met Moses, he gave him instructions to build the tabernacle. God gave specific instructions on how the tabernacle should be built and what should go in it. Tabernacle would be like a big tent that the Israelites can carry with them and set it up wherever they settle down. That would be the place where God met with His people. So, when Moses came down the mountain, he gathered the entire community together and told them everything God had instructed. Moses asked them to bring precious metals like gold, silver, and bronze; material like blue, purple, scarlet yarn, linen, goat hair, animals' skins, wood, oil, spices along with gemstones.

Moses told the community that the Lord had chosen Bezalel and Oholiab for their artistic craftmanship and given them the ability to teach others all the skills required in building the tabernacle. All who were willing brought in things they had which they had and soon the craftsman told Moses that the people are bringing more than what was required for making the Tabernacle. Then, Moses informed people to stop bringing their offerings.

They built the tabernacle just as God had instructed. They made the Tabernacle, the curtain/veil, the upright frames made of acacia wood. They also made an ark, a table, a lampstand, and other things God wanted them to do. Every object was made for a special purpose exactly as God had commanded. They also made the bronze basin for washing, everything needed for the courtyard, the priestly garments. Moses inspected the tabernacle when all their work was completed. When the work was completed, God told Moses how the tabernacle had to be set up. God told him to anoint the tabernacle and everything in it and consecrate it so that it would be holy. Anoint means "to pour oil on." God told Moses to bring Aaron and his sons to the entrance of the tabernacle.

Moses told Aaron along with his sons to come to the entrance to the tent of the Meeting and wash them with water and anointed Aaron to be a priest. Aaron's sons were also anointed to serve God as priests. Moses did exactly what God told him to do, and the tabernacle was finally completed.

God had led the Israelites from a cloud, and the cloud covered the tabernacle which meant that God's glory filled the tabernacle. God had made a sign for the people: If the cloud covered the tabernacle, the people would stay where they were. When the cloud lifted from the tabernacle, the Israelites would have to move and take the tabernacle with them. By day the Lord went ahead of them in a pillar of cloud to guide them on their way and by night in a pillar of fire to give them light so that they could travel by day or night.

God gave the Israelites all the instructions they needed to make the tabernacle and everything in it. God did not give them instructions in part but gave them all that they needed to know and all they had to do was to follow the instruction step by step. They had nothing to figure out by themselves, they got the complete blue print on what they had to do. The only thing they had to do is to follow the instructions without exceptions. And God dwelled among the Israelites and showed them when they had to stay and when they had to move and every Israelite could see the glory of God during the time. They did not have a GPS then to show them which direction they had to go nor a weather app to know the climate. All they had to do was to follow where God was taking them to the promised land!

****

****

"Exodus 40:38
"So the cloud of the Lord was over the Tabernacle by day, and fire was in the cloud by night, in the sight of all the house of Israel during all their travels""

****

****

"The reason why God instructed the Israelites to build a Tabernacle was because he wanted to dwell with them. We know that God never wants to leave us alone. In order to save us, God sent his only begotten son to the world to dwell with us. When Jesus was taken up to the heaven, he gave us the Holy Spirit to be with us so we would be.

Do you feel that you are all alone sometimes? Jesus has promised that he will never leave us nor forsake us at all times. Remember the situation doesn't change his promise. He is the same yesterday, today and forever"

Identify the different articles and parts in the Tabernacle of God in the crossword.

Tabernacle

```
F E L L V U W Q W E D H J G J O X F F T K G E R
P H O I H J B F O A F O H O C L U L B O J L H W
V D C N R R Z R N C C D E L B A T N M C Z B K S
W G K E O T S R I E C A C A L T A R V C L V F X
A F G N O S N W Y J E L C V I B M J O U W H S X
S H X Y A H E H B E O A T I T Z Q E U R X L X I
P J B C H H E J U N G M C T A H N D W T R Y G U
A Y F C M Z R I A S W P R H O W B V W A X G O A
M G A P K D C Y J T T F B E N A O E W I L B Z M
O H C R L A S K H L U Q I R J M A O X N X Z P I
J K B O N F Z M H W E C T V Z X U Z D S F O G M
H Z G W P X W M N Q Q G E Z G U R N T G V D B Z
B S I Z O L S G T C I E G K Q Z G T S T C V B J
X W S R N O C I Z I B U C K N S O L P N R Z B J
L S O O Y M D S L F D L K Y Q C F R I P U U N K
B S A I Q O V F B V A Q Z P P V X Y Y B D J O Y
X R F L S X D J R S E U I B O U Q N F K A K M C
N F O O R A A L P A G R S L A M P S T A N D I A
T G F N G B R S X F M B Y H F T J F L R A O F U
E M E B Z D F K V B U E T H M J K T L X T Y X W
N G Y N U E B R M B B K S K G J D A W Z C X L J
T P L E Q J U V U C O K A W W W Y T H F D S A C
V Q H M Q O F L R N R W A N E T A E S Y C R E M
T A B E R N A C L E A R V Y A Q Q G N F H D S I
```

acaciawood   altar   ark   bronze

clasps   court   curtains   gold

lamp   lampstand   linen   mercy-seat

oil   screens   silver   tabernacle

table   tent   wood frames   yarn

Source: https://wordmint.com/public_puzzles/482494

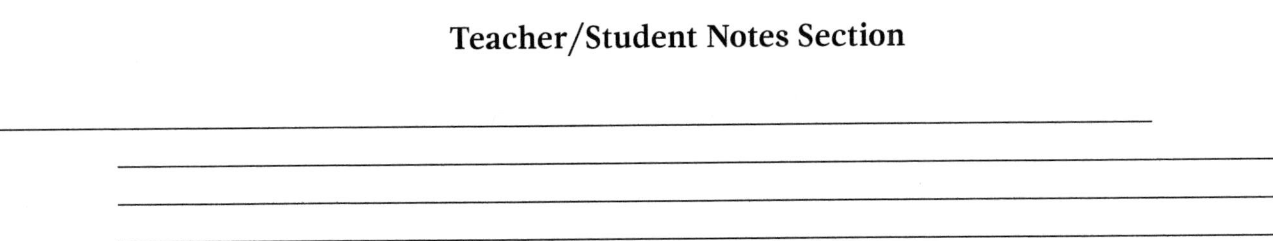

Teacher/Student Notes Section

Prayer

Ask one of the children in the group if she/he would like to lead the class in prayer (to pray for their classmates, family, church, teachers and pastors, and on what they learnt).

CHAPTER TWENTY-TWO

SACRIFICES - THE SHADOW

Session Starter

Take a clear glass and add some water to it. Then add some oil to the water and mix them well together. Let it settle, ask the children to observe what happens. Discuss water as the world and oil as Christians.

Leviticus 1-27
(Encourage children to open their bibles to the story portion)

Explain

The people set up the Tabernacle as how God commanded and God gave them instructions on how they have to make offerings and sacrifices. Sacrifices were necessary because no one could keep God's Laws perfectly. When Moses was with God on Mt. Sinai, he gave them laws. God is holy and cannot be around us. God gave them rules about offerings. Offerings are gifts that people give to God like money, food, animal or precious stones or metals. When they felt sorry for a sin, they could offer God a sin offering. The ones God discussed were Burnt Offering, Grain Offering, Fellowship Offering, Sin Offering and Guilt Offering.

God gave rules about how the priests should be making the sacrifices that God had mentioned. Since the priests took care of the tabernacle and they were the ones who taught people about God's rules for living holy lives. Aaron and his sons were chosen to serve as priests.

God also spoke about the Day of Atonement which would happen once a year. The people needed atonement for their sin in order to make the relationship right with God. The priest is to take the blood of an animal into the most holy place inside the tabernacle where he sprinkled the blood on the mercy seat of the ark of the covenant. The Lord gave them instructions not to lie, steal, deceive one another and to obey the rules.

He also mentioned about not eating fat and forbidden blood, the share of the priests and the ordination of Aaron and His sons. The Lord then told Moses and Aaron about what they can and cannot eat (clean and unclean food) The Lord also spoke about the regulations about infectious skin diseases. He gave punishments for sin, rules for priests and unacceptable sacrifices.

The Lord also spoke about the appointed feasts of the Lord, which the priests had to proclaim as sacred assemblies. The Sabbath, The Passover and unleavened bread, first fruits, feast of weeks, the feast of trumpets, Day of atonement, Feast of the tabernacle, Sabbath Year and the year of Jubilee. He finally also spoke about the reward for obedience and punishment for disobedience and redeeming what is the Lord's.

When you commit a crime, you don't get let out of jail because you are sorry. Justice requires you to pay for what you did. Therefore, the Israelites couldn't just walk in and have fellowship with the Lord. So, they had to sacrifice animals to atone for their sins. These sacrifices cost dearly. The farm animal was a considerable contribution as they had to give out their very best animal, best quality grain which taught them to show the importance of God in their lives.

Why did God require a blood sacrifice? Animals did no wrong, but still they had to die for no wrong of theirs (when they were sacrificed). Jesus Christ also did no wrong but willingly gave himself to die for us on the cross of Calvary

(1 Tim 2:6 & 2 Corin 5:21) According to the law almost everything is purified with blood and without shedding of blood there is no forgiveness (Heb 9:22).

Why did God give rules for sacrifice? God gave rules so that Israel (God's people) could make their relationship right with God. He told them how to worship Him and to be forgiven. During the time of worship and celebration during the feasts and celebration people went without doing work. They had to sacrifice the best animal or the grain during the harvest. This shows that they depended on God first before anything and loved him.

****

Memory Verse

****

"Leviticus 20:7
Consecrate yourselves and be holy, because I am the Lord your God. Keep my decrees and follow them.
I am the Lord, who makes you holy."

****

****

"The book of Leviticus contains many rules for Israelites, but we do not obey all the rules mentioned in the book like the different sacrifices mentioned in the book because we trust Jesus, who took all our sin on him. The Israelites had to make different sacrifices at different intervals of time.

Jesus shed his blood on the cross to pay for all our sins. He is our High Priest who is holy, blameless, pure and unlike the other high priests, he need not offer sacrifices for his own sins and then for the others. He sacrificed his life for our sins once for all (Heb 7: 26-27)."

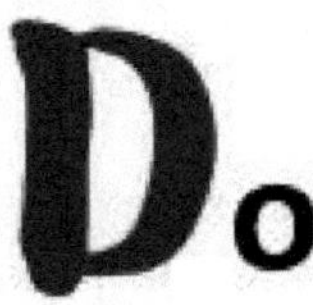

Food for thought:

What do you think an athelete would give up? May be free time, hanging out with friends, icecream, burgers, sleeping in late. Is it possible to achieve something in life without sacrificing something? This is called sacrifice.

If given a choice what would you like to sacrifice or give up for Lord? Talk about what the kids could give up for God.

Teacher/Student Notes Section

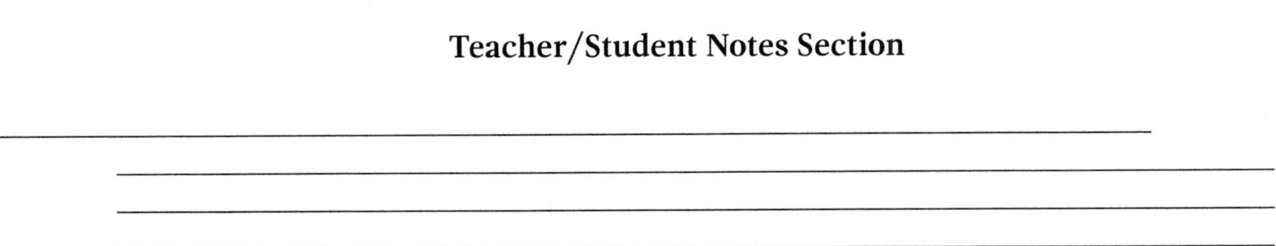

Prayer

Ask one of the children in the group if she/he would like to lead the class in prayer (to pray for their classmates, family, church, teachers and pastors, and on what they learnt).

CHAPTER TWENTY-THREE

WORSHIP THE LORD GOD ONLY

Session Starter

Talk to the children about the desert and the journey of the Israelites. Talk about how hot the days and how cold the nights would be. They had to keep moving whenever God moved...No entertainment most of all... Discuss with the children and get their views.

Deuteronomy 1; 3:23-4:40
(Encourage children to open their bibles to the story portion)

Explain

The Lord our God said to his people at Horeb, "You have stayed enough on the mountain long enough, so break the camp and advance into the hill country of the Amorites, to the mountains of Arabah, Negev, Land of Canaanites, Lebanon and the rivers of Euphrates. He said that I have given you this land, go and take possession of the land the Lord had promised to give to your fathers and their descendants.

Since a lot of Moses's time was spent on solving the problems and resolving disputes by himself in the Israelite community, he chose some wise understanding and respected men from each of the tribes and set them as commanders/ judges over them. And they were instructed to bring to Moses any difficult case they had.

Then the people came to Moses and said "Let us send men ahead to spy out the land and to bring back a report for us. Since the idea seemed good, Moses chose 12 people one from each tribe to go out as spies and they came back with a good report that the land was good.

The people were unwilling, unbelieving and grumbled in their tents and said "The people are stronger and taller than we are, the cities are large, with walls up to the sky" Moses encouraged the people and told them not to be terrified not to be afraid of them and that they had seen how they were delivered from the land of Egypt. Still, they did not trust in God despite seeing the Lord's hand lead them through the pillar of fire during the night and pillar of cloud during the day. So, the Lord was angry and said that only Joshua and Caleb would be able to set their feet on the promised land.

The Lord became angry with Moses as well and told him that he wouldn't be able to enter the land. But then the people cried out to the Lord saying that they have sinned and that they would go and fight just as the Lord commanded.

The Lord told Moses to tell the Israelites not to go and fight now but they wouldn't listen but they did and were defeated by the Amorites. Moses then pleaded with the Lord but the Lord told him not to speak about it anymore.

Moses told the Israelites to follow the decrees and laws that the Lord had told them to do. Watch yourselves closely so that you do not forget the things your eyes have seen or let them slip from your heart as long as you live. Teach them to your children and to their children after them. They were also told not to indulge in any form of idol worship and that if they seek the Lord with all their heart, they would find him, that he is a merciful God. He made the people hear his voice to discipline them and to know that there is no other God and all may go well with them and their children if they kept the decrees and the commandments.

All through that time the Lord had been taking care of the Israelites. When the Lord promised them to take them to the promised Land, the people were unwilling and rebelled against the command of the Lord and grumbled in their tents and complained saying "The Lord hates us; so, he brought us out of Egypt to deliver us in the hands of the Amorites to destroy us." ***What do you do when you are going through a desert in your life (difficult situation)? Do you complain, grumble and complain like the Israelites or the 10 spies or are you like Joshua and Caleb who trusted in the Lord's promise to his people.***

Remember that our God is a merciful God his anger lasts only a moment but his favour lasts a lifetime and you will find him if you seek him with all your heart! Know that whatever situation you are going through, you are never alone. The Lord is just a prayer away!!

****

Memory Verse

****

"Deuteronomy 4:31
The Lord your God is a merciful God; he will not abandon or destroy you or forget the covenant with your forefathers, which he confirmed to them by oath."

****

Christ Connect

****

"Our Lord is a good and gracious God who did not want us to perish so sent his only begotten son. He also has given us laws and decrees that we need to keep so he would bless us. No matter which season or situation you are in life, God is near you and he is able to deliver you. Through his grace and mercy you will be made worthy and clean to inherit eternal life."

Do

Talk about the Map:
The journey of Israel from Egypt to Canaan

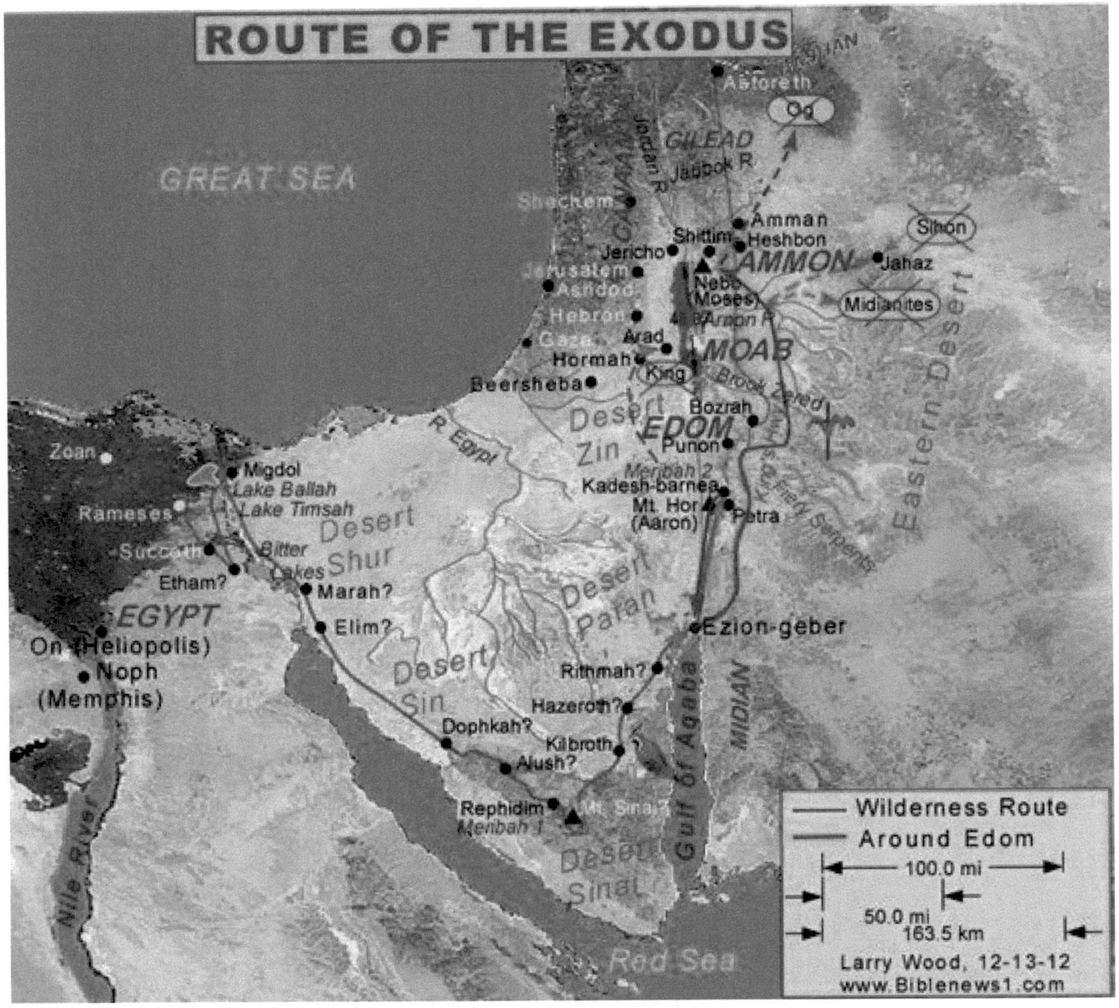

Source: https://in.pinterest.com/pin/79376012175182276/

Teacher/Student Notes Section

____

____

____

____

Prayer

Ask one of the children in the group if she/he would like to lead the class in prayer (to pray for their classmates, family, church, teachers and pastors, and on what they learnt).

CHAPTER TWENTY-FOUR

GOD REMINDS HIS COVENANT TO ISRAELITES

Session Starter

Can you ask the kids to talk about their answered prayers. Ask them to write it down and discuss about it. See how many kids can remember.

Deuteronomy 5:1-6:25; 8:1-11:1, 26-28
(Encourage children to open their bibles to the story portion)

Explain

Moses reminded the people that he stood face to face with the Lord on the mountain and how they were afraid and did not go up the mountain, He told them that they should learn and follow the decrees and the laws the Lord had given to them. He told them of all the 10 commandments that the Lord had written with his hand on 2 stone tablets and had given to him.

The people had told Moses that he can speak to the Lord on their behalf and tell them whatever instructions he had for them and they were ready to obey them. He told them "Be careful to do what the Lord had commanded so that they will prosper and prolong your days in the land that you will possess"

He also said told them to" Love the Lord your God with all your heart and with all your soul and with all your strength" He instructed them to impress the instructions in the heart of their children, how they are to talk to them when you sit with them and to tie them as symbols on their hands and foreheads. If your children ask them what is the meaning of the decrees and laws, they had to tell them of how the Lord delivered them from Egypt from slavery and delivered them. And that they have to fear the Lord, serve him only, keep the laws and remember all that the Lord had done for them in their lives.

He also reminded the people of how the Lord had led them through their journey in the desert how he humbled them, fed them with manna and taught them that man did not live by bread alone but by every word that comes from the mouth of the Lord and how their clothes did not wear out and their feet not swelling during these 40 years. He told them about how they had provoked the Lord to anger in the desert by making a Golden Calf and how angry Moses was when he saw people worshipping it and he broke the tablets and then how he had humbled and cried out to the Lord so that He would forgive them.

The Lord then told Moses to make 2 stone tablets exactly similar to the ones like last time and to put it in the chest. He told them that if they follow the commands of the Lord then it will be a blessing and will be a curse if they disobey the commands that the Lord had given them.

God had made a promise to the Israelites that if they obeyed his laws and decrees, he would bless them. Though God can, he does not force us into obeying his laws, but is pleased when we obey him by choice. God wants us to obey him not by compulsion nor fear because we love him. ***How can we show God that we love him?***

Sometimes we think that our hard work had brought us to where we are, but in reality, it is God who provides and protects us. ***Do you always give God the credit for who he is and what he does?*** God had promised the Israelites that he will be their God and protect and provide for all their needs and that they were to follow his commandments. But they broke the promise, still God remained faithful and he never broke his promise to them.

God had promised the Israelites that he will be their God and protect and provide for all their needs and that they were to follow his commandments. Even though the people broke their promise, God remained faithful and he never broke his promise to them. Think about it. ***Are you like Israelites?*** Moses prayed to the Lord for the people's sins. Do you? The Lord said that he humbled the people to test them, fed them with manna, their clothes never wore out nor their feet swell during their journey in the desert. ***Why do you think you are going through a difficult situation in your life?***

****

Memory Verse

****

"Deuteronomy 6:4,5
Hear O Israel: The Lord our God, the Lord is one. Love the Lord your God with all your heart and with all your soul and with all your strength."

****

****

"The Israelites had the greatest privilege of being the children of God; to be led, guided and fed by God himself! The people had to obey all the laws without exception. But now as Christians we are under grace. Rom 6:14. We are reconciled with God by grace alone. Jesus on the cross, shed his precious blood to give us sinners forgiveness. We are sinners by habit and are made new creation by God because they are given the gift of the holy spirit which seeks God and his righteousness and has delivered us from our sins. We are no longer a slave to sin. Our master is Lord who is able to bring us back from sin through the blood of Christ and the power of the Holy Spirit."

Love the Lord your God

Challenge yourself! Complete the word search in under five minutes!

F	H	Y	X	H	N	L	I	I	Z	O	K	K	H	F
I	Z	C	E	Y	U	E	O	E	A	G	L	U	T	P
K	S	A	I	O	E	A	R	K	X	N	W	V	G	T
T	R	R	S	V	F	B	I	D	H	C	H	S	N	R
T	Q	V	A	U	I	Z	O	T	L	E	I	C	E	R
C	K	X	P	E	R	X	Y	W	S	I	Q	Q	R	C
X	P	F	I	K	L	P	S	I	Q	H	H	S	T	D
C	C	W	H	F	F	L	M	B	L	A	W	C	S	T
C	M	T	P	H	W	O	U	V	L	W	S	U	T	Q
Y	M	O	N	O	R	E	T	U	E	D	I	E	S	B
P	D	W	W	P	Z	Z	R	S	X	Z	R	O	H	T
T	S	A	Q	L	T	S	M	N	G	I	A	F	E	U
D	R	O	L	C	U	F	P	R	A	Y	E	R	M	A
X	M	E	A	L	F	A	T	R	S	K	H	D	A	G
C	E	K	B	B	G	O	O	P	R	H	M	X	B	U

CHILDREN	DEUTERONOMY	HEAR
HEART	ISRAEL	LORD
OBEY	PRAYER	PROMISE
SHEMA	SOUL	STRENGTH

Source: https://static1.squarespace.com/static/547ce2c7e4b0e777512bbfbb/t/5e75a8946e27d0443d2fbd4b/1584769174446/Sunday+22nd+Kidspoint+Worksheets.pdf

Teacher/Student Notes Section

____

____

____

____

Prayer

Ask one of the children in the group if she/he would like to lead the class in prayer (to pray for their classmates, family, church, teachers and pastors, and on what they learnt).

CHAPTER TWENTY-FIVE

JOSHUA AND CALEB

Session Starter

Choose a volunteer and ask her/him to face away from the class. The other kids then help choose an item in the room. The volunteer is invited to figure out what the object is. The rest of the kids cannot say anything. They only clap if the volunteer starts going toward the object. The closer the volunteer gets, the faster the kids should clap. When he/she identifies the object, the class responds by standing and clapping. Say God's people were looking for clues about a place that had been chosen for them to live. They had a choice to make based on what they found.

Numbers 13:1-14:38
(Encourage children to open their bibles to the story portion)

Explain

God's people had travelled out of Egypt and were almost to the promised land. God told Moses, "Send men to go look at the land of Canaan. I am giving this land to My people." So Moses sent out one leader from each family tribe. Two of the men who went were named Joshua and Caleb. Moses told the men, "See what the land is like and what the people who live there are like." Moses had a lot of questions: Is the land good or bad? Are the cities like camps or forts? Is the land good for farming? Are there trees in it? Moses told the men, "Have courage!"

So the men went and looked at the land. They travelled around the land for 40 days. They cut down a bunch of grapes in the valley. The grapes were so big the bunch had to be carried on a pole. They brought different kinds of fruit back to Moses, Aaron, and the Israelite people. "The land is very nice," they said, "but the people living in the land are strong. The cities they live in are big and protected." But Caleb said, "We must go up and make the land ours! We can do it with God's help!" But other men said, "We cannot go up against those people! We looked like grasshoppers compared to them!"All of the Israelites started to cry. "Let's pick a new leader and go back to Egypt!" they said. Joshua and Caleb said to the Israelites, "If the Lord is pleased with us, He will give it to us. Don't be afraid of the people living in the land; God is with us!"

God spoke to Moses: "How long will these people dislike Me? How long will they not trust Me?" Moses said, "Please forgive their sin. I know You are patient, loving, and forgiving." God said, "Since you have asked, I will forgive them. But no one who complained against Me will get to see the promised land." God said the Israelites would wander in the wilderness and would not enter the promised land, and that Only Joshua, Caleb, and the children of Israel would one day enter the land.

- What were some of the good things Joshua and the other spies saw in the land?

____
____

- What made most of the spies afraid?

____
____

- Which spy thought they should go and take the land?

____
____

- Whom did Joshua remind the people would help them take the land? Did the Israelites' choice please God?"

____
____

- What is God calling you to do that you are already doing or not doing?

____
____

- Consider areas of your life where you commonly struggle to obey God. What are you believing or not believing that is causing you to not trust God in this area of your life?

____
____

****

Memory Verse

****

"Numbers 14:6-8

Joshua ...and Caleb ... said ... "The land we passed through ... is exceedingly good. 8 If the Lord is pleased with us, he will lead us into that land, a land flowing with milk and honey, and will give it to us."

****

Christ Connect

****

"The Israelites turned away from God because they did not trust Him. Jesus always trusted God. He took the punishment we deserve for turning away from God. When we trust in Jesus, God forgives our sin and gives us life with Him forever. We need to trust in the Lord with all your heart, and should not rely on your own understanding (Proverbs 3:5)."

Do

Divide the group into pairs, and have one teammate blindfolded. The blindfolded teammate raises their hands in front of their shoulders, hands adjacent and thumbs almost touching, to create a bumper. The other teammate is the driver and must steer the car by directing them with their shoulders. Have a facilitator give traffic directions, like school zone, red light, green light, etc.

Joshua and Caleb put their faith and trust in God and His strength and power, they were the two that believed and had faith that God would do what He said and lead them into the land that He promised. The other spies saw how big everything in the land was rather than looking at how big God is. God wants us to be like Joshua and Caleb and have faith in God. They saw the possibilities instead of the problems, God instead of giants, and victory instead of defeat.

Teacher/Student Notes Section

Prayer

Ask one of the children in the group if she/he would like to lead the class in prayer (to pray for their classmates, family, church, teachers and pastors, and on what they learnt).

CHAPTER TWENTY-SIX

The Bronze Snake

Session Starter

Grateful or grumbling. Guide boys and girls to sit in a circle.

SAY: I am going to announce a scenario. If the situation would make you unhappy, cross your arms and say, "Grumble, grumble, grumble." If it would make you happy, stand and shout, "Hurray!" Call out several scenarios. For example: A heavy snowstorm cancels school for a week. Your dad asks you to take out the trash. You have to share your room with your little sister.

SAY: In today's Bible story, the Israelites forgot all the wonderful things God had done for them, and they complained. Do you think God was happy to hear them complain? Listen to today's Bible story to find out what happened.

Numbers 20:1-20,21:4-9
(Encourage children to open their bibles to the story portion)

The Israelites refused to go into the promised land, so God punished them and made them wander in the wilderness. The Israelites grumbled and complained. When the Israelites set up camp, they complained that they did not have water to drink. God told Moses and Aaron to stand in front of all the people and speak to a rock. God said water would come out of the rock. Moses called the people together, but instead of talking to the rock, Moses hit the rock two times with his staff. The water came out, but God was angry that Moses and Aaron disobeyed Him. God said Moses and Aaron would not lead the Israelites into the promised land. The Israelites continued through the wilderness.

Moses sent messengers to ask the king of Edom if the Israelites could travel through his land. But the people of Edom replied, "No! If you come to our land, we will fight you!" So the Israelites had to travel around Edom. The journey was long, and they grumbled and complained. "Why have you led us from Egypt to die in the wilderness?" they asked. "We have no bread or water! The food we have is no good!" God sent poisonous snakes that bit the Israelites, and many of the people died.

They realized they had sinned by complaining to God, so they told Moses, "We know we have sinned. Please ask God to take the snakes away." Moses interceded for the people. He spoke to God for them. Then God told Moses, "Make a snake image and put it on a pole. When anyone who is bitten looks at it, he will recover." Moses made a bronze snake and mounted it on a pole. Whenever someone was bitten, that person looked at the bronze snake, and he recovered.

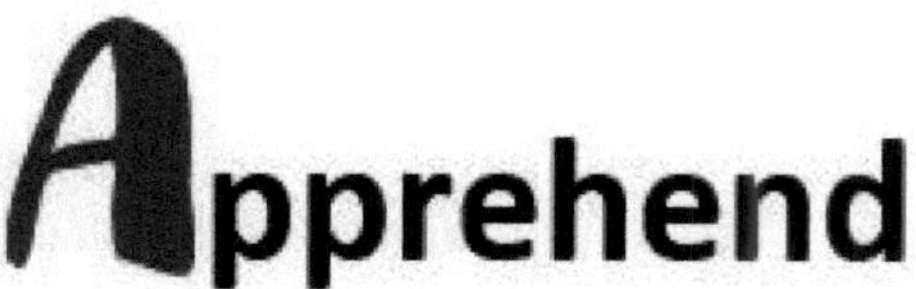

Ask kids if they have ever heard the word gospel. Clarify that the word gospel means "good news." It is the message about Christ, the kingdom of God, and salvation. Use the following guide to share the gospel with kids.

- God rules. Explain to kids that the Bible tells us God created everything, and He is in charge of everything. Invite a volunteer to read Genesis 1:1 from the Bible. Read Revelation 4:11 or Colossians 1:16-17 aloud and explain what these verses mean.
- We sinned. Tell kids that since the time of Adam and Eve, everyone has chosen to disobey God. (Romans 3:23) The Bible calls this sin. Because God is holy, God cannot be around sin. Sin separates us from God and deserves God's punishment of death. (Romans 6:23)
- God provided. Choose a child to read John 3:16 aloud. Say that God sent His Son, Jesus, the perfect solution to our sin problem, to rescue us from the punishment we deserve. It's something we, as sinners, could never earn on our own. Jesus alone saves us. Read and explain Ephesians 2:8-9.
- Jesus gives. Share with kids that Jesus lived a perfect life, died on the cross for our sins, and rose again. Because Jesus gave up His life for us, we can be welcomed into God's family for eternity. This is the best gift ever! Read Romans 5:8; 2 Corinthians 5:21; or 1 Peter 3:19.
- We respond. Tell kids that they can respond to Jesus. Read Romans 10:9-10,13. Review these aspects of our response: Believe in your heart that Jesus alone saves you through what He's already done on the cross. Repent, turning from self and sin to Jesus. Tell God and others that your faith is in Jesus. Offer to talk with any child who is interested in responding to Jesus.

****

Memory Verse

****

"John 3:14,15

Just as Moses lifted up the snake in the wilderness, so the Son of Man must be lifted up, 15 that everyone who believes may have eternal life in him."

****

Christ Connect

****

"Though God cared, nurtured, protected, and provided for Israel in the wilderness, Israelites murmured and complaint against God. God was angry with Israel because of their sin, and so He sent poisonous snakes to punish them. However, God is just and merciful and so he provided a choice and way Israel could be saved from dying even if bitten by snake; and that was to look at the snake on the pole and live.

Mankind is born in sin, and so are separated from God. However, our merciful and just God has given us a choice – that anyone who looks to Jesus on the cross and accepts Jesus as the savior will be restored back in the relationship with God and will live forever with God.

The choice is given to us, let us always choose Jesus!”

Do

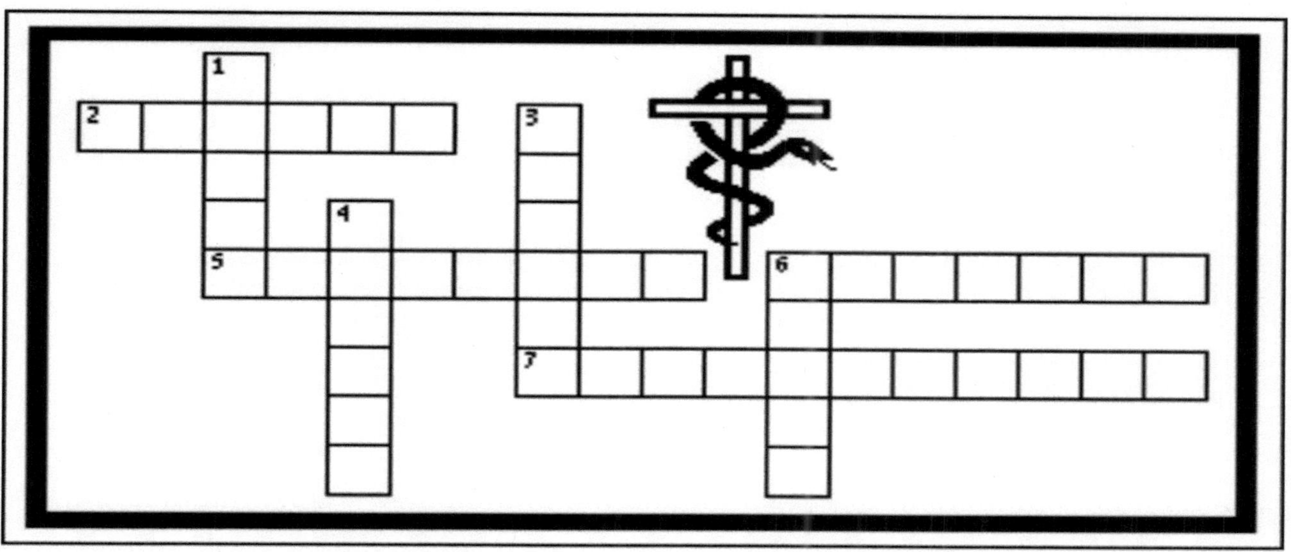

1 DOWN "And as _____ lifted up the serpent in the wilderness, even so must the Son of Man be lifted up." JOHN 3:14

7 ACROSS The children of Israel "journeyed from Mount Hor by the Way of the Red Sea, to go around the land of Edom; and the soul of the people became very _____ on the way." **NUMBERS 21:4**

6 ACROSS "And the people spoke against God and against Moses: 'Why have you brought us up out of Egypt to die in the wilderness? For there is no food and no water, and our soul _____ this worthless bread.' " **NUMBERS 21:5**

5 ACROSS "So the LORD sent fiery _____ among the people, and they bit the people; and many of the people of Israel died." **NUMBERS 21:6**

3 DOWN "Therefore the people came to Moses, and said, 'We have _____ for we have spoken against the LORD and against you; pray to the LORD that He take away the serpents from us.' " **NUMBERS 21:7**

4 DOWN "So Moses _____ for the people." **NUMBERS 21:7**

6 DOWN "Then the LORD said to Moses, 'Make a fiery serpent, and set it on a pole; and it shall be that everyone who is bitten, when he _____ at it, shall live." **NUMBERS 21:8**

2 ACROSS "So Moses made a _____ serpent, and put it on a pole; and so it was, if a serpent had bitten anyone, when he looked at the bronze serpent, he lived." **NUMBERS 21:9**

Teacher/Student Notes Section

____

____

____

____

Prayer

Ask one of the children in the group if she/he would like to lead the class in prayer (to pray for their classmates, family, church, teachers and pastors, and on what they learnt).

CHAPTER TWENTY-SEVEN

Jericho And The Promised Land

Session Starter

Song:

My God is so big! So strong and so mighty.
There's nothing my God cannot do (clap-clap).
My God is so big! So strong and so mighty.
There's nothing my God cannot do (clap-clap).
The mountains are his and the valleys are his
and the trees are his handiwork too.
My God is so big! So strong and so mighty.
There's nothing my God cannot do for you.

Joshua 1-4, 6
(Encourage children to open their bibles to the story portion)

When Moses died, Joshua became the leader of the Israelites. God told Joshua it was time to go into the land of Canaan, the land God promised to give Abraham's family. Other people lived in the land, so the Israelites had to defeat them. The opposition was tough, but God encouraged Joshua to be strong and courageous and promised that He would be with him wherever he goes. Joshua sent two spies into Jericho to check it out. They stayed at the house of a woman named Rahab (RAY hab). The king of Jericho heard the spies were with Rahab, so Rahab hid the men on her roof to keep them safe. Rahab had heard what God did to Pharaoh and believed in God. She wanted to help His people. The spies promised to keep Rahab and her family safe when the Israelites came into the city. Rahab tied a bright red rope in her window so the Israelites would know which house she lived in. The spies left Jericho. Now the Israelites travelled toward the Jordan River, which separated them from the promised land. They camped next to the wide, deep river.

God gave instructions to Joshua and the other leaders. God was going to help the Israelites cross the river. The people got ready to cross. The priests carried the ark of the covenant to the edge of the water. Joshua said, "God is with us. He will defeat our enemies." Then the priests stepped into the water, and the river stopped. All the people crossed the Jordan on dry ground. Joshua told the people to take 12 stones from the river to set up as a reminder that God stopped the water and helped them cross the river. When the Israelites were all on the other side, the water started to flow again. Next, God told Joshua, "March around the city one time each day for six days. On the seventh day, march around the city seven times, and the priests should blow the trumpets. Then all the people should shout, and the walls of Jericho will fall down. The Israelites can then go into the city and conquer it." Joshua did what God said. Every day for six days, the Israelites marched around the city. On the seventh day, they marched around the city seven times. Then Joshua said, "Shout, for the Lord has given you the city!" So the people shouted, and the wall fell down. The Israelites went into the city and captured it.

There were many rich things in Jericho. There were gold and silver and other riches. Joshua told the Israelites not to keep anything for themselves. Any riches that were found would belong to the Lord. They put it into the treasury in the tabernacle of the Lord. They destroyed everything in the city, Joshua remembered that the woman, Rahab, had protected the spies when they had come to Jericho. She had put a red cord in her window just as the spies had told her. When the Israelites saw the cord, they let Rahab and her family leave the city safely.

Who fought the battle of Jericho? God fought for His people and handed Jericho over to the Israelites. Who meets our greatest need? (Jesus meets our greatest need—to be saved from our sin. We can trust Him for our salvation.) Jesus told His followers in Matthew 6 that following God's commands and seeking His righteousness is what they should focus on. God will provide for His people's needs when they follow Him. Joshua's strong faith in God led him to obey, no matter how illogical God's command might be. Joshua also drew from the past, remembering the impossible deeds God had accomplished through Moses. Do you trust God with your life? Have you forgotten how he brought you through past troubles? God has not changed and he never will. He promises to be with you wherever you go.

"God is going to ask us and lead us down paths that sometimes are not going to make sense to us in our human wisdom. In that tug of war between the flesh and the spirit you should always side with God. He knows what's best for us, much like a parent knows what's best for a child."

****

Memory Verse

****

"Joshua 1:9

Have I not commanded you? Be strong and courageous. Do not be afraid; do not be discouraged, for the Lord your God will be with you wherever you go.""

****

****

"God fought for His people and led them into the promised land. Just as the Lord defeated Jericho for the Israelites, Jesus defeats His enemies and leads believers into the promised land of eternity."

Do

Joshua Obeys God at Jericho
—Joshua 5

Seven Times Around

God told Joshua to march his army around the city of Jericho once each day for six days. On the seventh day, they were to march around the city seven times. The seventh time around, the priests blew their trumpets and the people shouted. To find out what happened then, circle every other letter beginning at start. Copy the letters onto the spaces below. The first circled letter is done for you.

A_ ____ ______ ___ ____

__________ ____ _______,

___ ______ _____.

Source: https://i.pinimg.com/originals/40/e8/e4/40e8e4186827217ed5203195cb8dea42.gif

Teacher/Student Notes Section

____

____

____

____

Prayer

Ask one of the children in the group if she/he would like to lead the class in prayer (to pray for their classmates, family, church, teachers and pastors, and on what they learnt).

CHAPTER TWENTY-EIGHT

THE DEFEAT OF AI

Session Starter

Form two teams of kids. Divide the room evenly with a masking tape line, and instruct teams to stand against a wall on opposite sides of the line. Place a ball for each team on the line. Call out the names of one kid from each team to run and "steal" her team's ball before the other person grabs hers. Lead kids to replace the balls, line up again, and play again. Play as time allows, choosing new kids each round.

You had to be fast and tricky to steal the ball. In real life, we know that stealing is wrong. No matter how fast or tricky you are, God always knows what you've done. Stealing is a sin and sin separates people from God. Listen to today's story to find out how one man's sin caused a big problem for God's people.

Joshua 7, 8
(Encourage children to open their bibles to the story portion)

Israel had entered in the promised as God had promised; under the leadership of Joshua. However, the land had to cleared off for habitation- which means Israel had a task at hand! They had to fight the enemies. God was with Israel, and He promised to fight for them. The Lord had helped the Israelites take over the city of Jericho. He had given them specific instructions on what they could take and what to destroy.

However, the Israelites did not obey God completely. They kept some things for themselves, and God knew. Now the time came for them to attack and conquest the city of Ai; Israel set out to fight Ai and thought God would back them up. However, God did not fight for them. The men of Ai chased away the Israelites, and some of the Israelites were killed. Now all the Israelites were afraid. Joshua was sad. He did not understand why Israel had lost the battle.

But God said to Joshua, "Israel has sinned. They took some of the things I told them not to. This is why they cannot defeat their enemies." God told Joshua how to deal with the people's sins. So the next day, the Israelites came together, and God showed Joshua which man had sinned. The man's name was Achan. Achan confessed that he had taken from Jericho a beautiful cloak, some pieces of silver, and a bar of gold. Achan had buried the things in his tent. So the people of Israel killed Achan and his family. After Achan was punished for his sin, God told Joshua to attack Ai again.

This time, God promised to give them victory over the city. Joshua gathered an army. He sent some of the armies out at night to lie in wait behind the city. Then early the next morning, the rest of the army went toward the city. The king of Ai saw them and sent out his men to fight them. When the enemy army got near, Joshua and the Israelites ran away, just as they had before. They pretended to be afraid, so the army of Ai chased them away from the city.

The people of Ai had no idea that Joshua had men hiding on the other side of the city. The army of Ai left the city completely unprotected. Joshua held out his sword, and the men who were hiding took over the city and set it on fire. This time, the Israelites did just what God said. The army of Ai realized that they were trapped, and the Israelites defeated them. Joshua built an altar to the Lord, where the Israelites sacrificed offerings to God. Joshua taught Israel and read aloud the words of the law Moses had commanded.

God's Plan for Me: Achan disobeyed God, and the punishment for Achan's sin was death. Explain that God was just to punish Achan in that way. The Bible says that the punishment for sin is death. Everyone who sins deserves to die. Have you ever received a punishment that did not seem to fit the wrong thing you did? That's the bad news.

The good news is that God's Son, Jesus, came to earth to die for our sins. He took the punishment we deserve when He died on the cross. When we trust in Jesus, God forgives our sin and gives us eternal life. Our faith in Him—not our obedience—gives us right standing with God. Because of our faith in Jesus, God is always with us and we are victorious over our enemies of sin and death.

The story of Achan demonstrates that God hates sin. (See Prov. 6:16-19.) God is just to punish sin. Here's the bad news: We are all sinners, and "the wages of sin is death," but here is the good news: "the gift of God is eternal life in Christ Jesus our Lord" (Rom. 6:23). God's presence with Israel was tied directly to their obedience to Him. It is our faith, not our obedience, that gives us right standing with God. Because of our faith in Jesus Christ, God is always with us and we are victorious over our enemies of sin and death.

****

Memory Verse

****

"Psalms 139: 2
You know when I sit and when I rise; you perceive my thoughts from afar. 3 You discern my going out and my lying down; you are familiar with all my ways."

****

****

"The punishment for Achan's sin was death. It seems harsh, but the Bible says that the wages of sin is death (Romans 6:23). Because we sin, we deserve to die too. Jesus came to die in our place. When we confess our sins and trust in Jesus, we are forgiven and are saved from eternal death and hell."

Activity

From the lesson learnt emphasize how God HATES sin. As a reminder students will make a tent. And on the tent they will write a reminder to themselves "As for me and my house we will serve the Lord"

<u>Materials to build the tent</u>

1. White 67 lb. Cardstock
2. Tent Pattern
3. Scissors
4. Glue
5. Paper Plates
6. Sand
7. Markers, Crayons, or Colored Pencils
8. Aluminum Foil

<u>Directions:</u>

1. Teachers will copy the tent pattern (as shown below) for each student on 67 lb. Cardstock.
2. Have students cut out the tent pattern on the solid black lines.
3. Allow students to color their tents using markers, crayons, or colored pencils.
4. Instruct them to fold on the dotted black lines.
5. Glue Tab A to Tab B and then glue Tab C to Tab D.
6. Glue tent onto a paper plate.
7. Have students spread glue on the paper plate and then sprinkle sand over the glue.
8. Allow students to write "As for me and my house we will serve the Lord" on top of it.

Joshua 7:1-26

TENT PATTERN

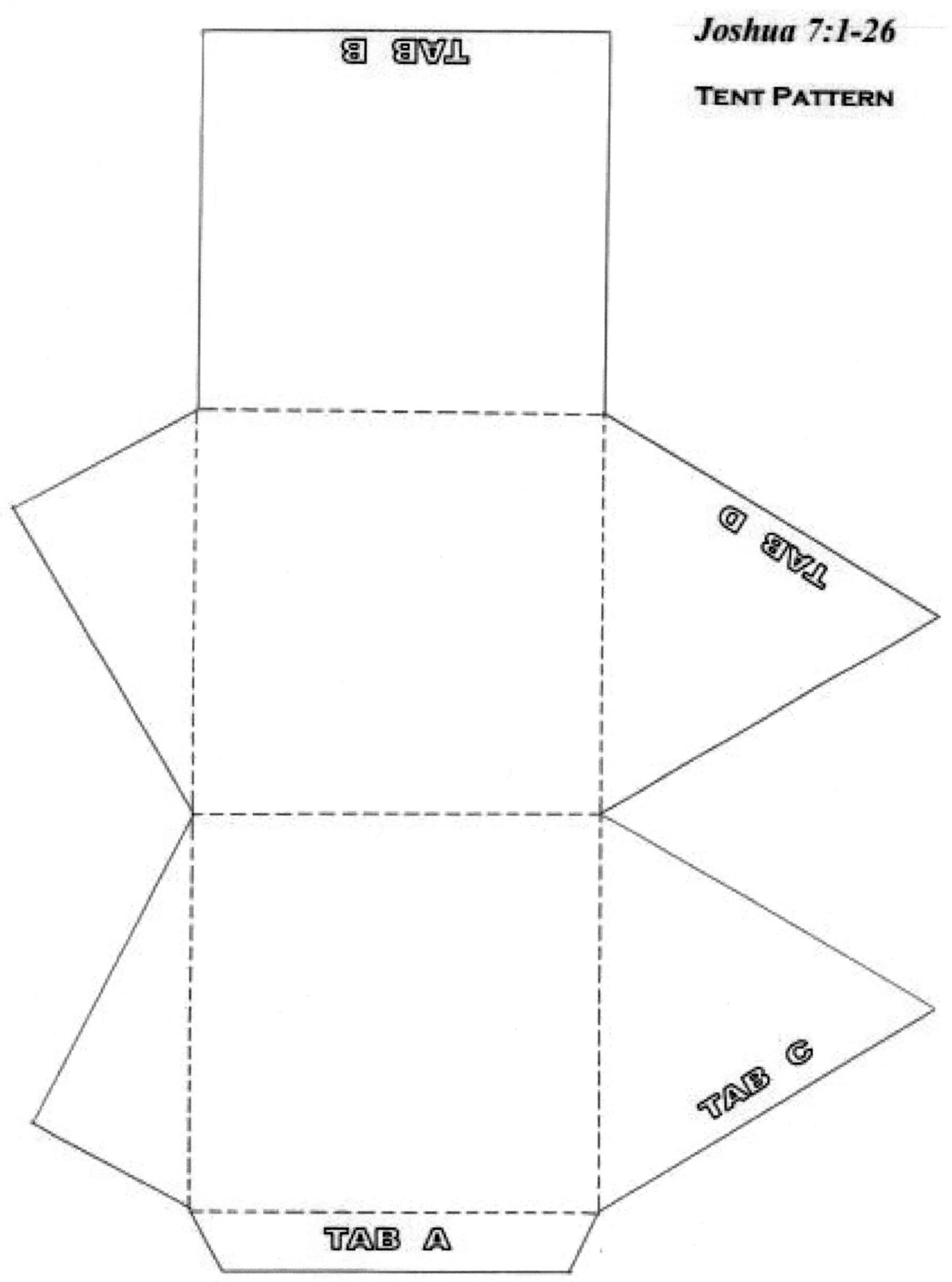

Source: https://freesundayschoolcurriculum.weebly.com/uploads/1/2/5/0/12503916/lesson_62_achans_sin.pdf

Discussion:

As students are constructing their tents, remind them that God told Joshua that he would not be with the Israelites anymore unless Joshua destroyed whatever was among them that had sinned. Help students realize that God takes sin very seriously. Because Achan sinned, he lost his life and almost caused the Israelites to loose favor with God for good. Encourage students to seek forgiveness when they sin.

Teacher/Student Notes Section

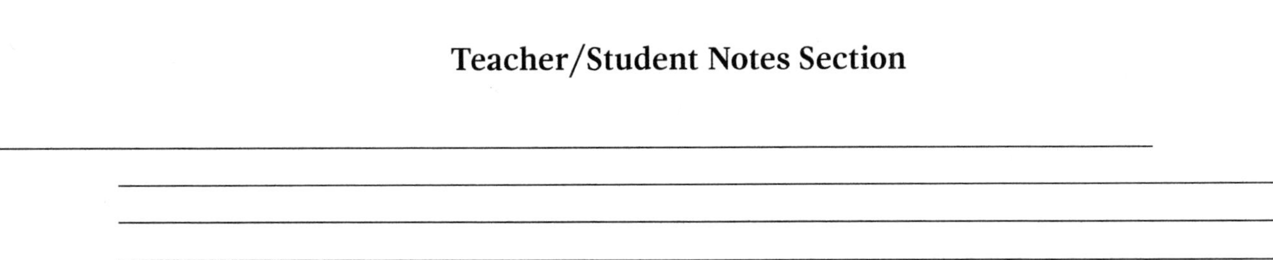

Prayer

Ask one of the children in the group if she/he would like to lead the class in prayer (to pray for their classmates, family, church, teachers and pastors, and on what they learnt).

CHAPTER TWENTY-NINE

Joshua's Last Words

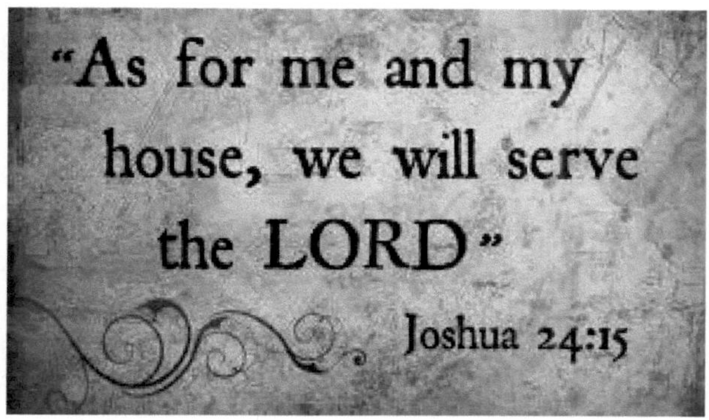

Session Starter

Message sent

Encourage the kids to sit in a circle while holding hands. Choose a volunteer. The volunteer will sit in the middle of the circle. Invite the volunteer to close her eyes while you tap the shoulder of one of the kids in the circle. Explain how that kid will "send a message" by squeezing the hand of the kid to his right. The kid to his right will then squeeze the hand of the kid to her right. This continues until the message is returned to the original sender. The volunteer in the middle is trying to "catch" the message as it travels by observing who is passing the message. If caught, the sender switches places with the volunteer. Otherwise, choose another volunteer and play again.

We have many ways to send a message. Near the end of his life, Joshua had an important message to send to the Israelites. Today, we will find out what he said.

Joshua 23:1-24:33
(Encourage children to open their bibles to the story portion)

After the great victories and wars at Jericho, Ai, and the kings of the land, God allowed the Israelites to rest from battles against their enemies.

Joshua was now old. He knew his last days were in, and so he gathered all the people of Israel to share with them some important things. Joshua said, "You have seen everything the LORD your God has done—He has fought your battles for you. All of the land that remains will be yours too. God will push back the people who live there and move them out of your sight. You will possess that land, just as the LORD your God promised you." "Therefore," Joshua continued, "be careful to obey everything that is in the book of the law of Moses. Do not turn aside from it; do not mix with the nations in this land or worship their gods. Cling to God, just as you have done. God fights for you! Be very careful, then, to love the LORD your God. If you disobey God, He will no longer help you win these battles. In fact, you will die here if you disobey Him." Joshua spoke more to the Israelites. He said, "I am going to die soon. All of you know in your hearts and souls that God has kept every one of His promises. But know for certain that if you disobey God, He will keep His promise to bring bad things upon you, and you will die in this land He has given to you."

Joshua reminded all the people about the things God had done for them in the past. Joshua reminded them of everything from when God called Abraham to leave his kindred and go to the land where God showed, and how God blessed Abraham with Isaac, the son of His promise.. and how God blessed Isaac with two sons, Jacob and Esau.

He reminded them that Jacob's children were in a time of slavery in Egypt and how God sent Moses and Aaron. Joshua told the people about how God had rescued the Israelites from the Egyptians, bringing them safely across the Red Sea and saving them from the Egyptians who were chasing them. Joshua reminded them of the many battles they had fought and won because God was fighting for them. God had done so many great things for His people! Joshua commanded the people, "Fear the LORD and worship Him. Joshua challenged the people and asked them whom they would want to worship the gods their ancestors worshiped of God Almighty Yahweh, and Joshua said, "As for my family and me, we will worship Yahweh." The people replied, "We will certainly not abandon the LORD to worship other gods! We know how much God has done for us, and we love Him!".

Joshua warned the people, "If you do abandon God to worship other gods, God will turn against you and harm you. He will destroy you after all of the good things He has done for you!" "No!" the people replied. "We will worship Yahweh!" On that day, Joshua made a covenant with the people. He wrote it down in the book of the law of God. He also took a large stone and set it up under an oak tree next to the sanctuary of the LORD. "You see this stone," Joshua said. "It will be a reminder of your duty to serve the LORD, who fulfilled every promise in bringing you into this land." Then Joshua sent the people away; each man went to the land he had inherited.

After these things, Joshua, son of Nun, died when he was 110 years old.

The Israelites decided to serve God first. We always put God first. Right? Have you ever had to make a choice between God and something else? Can anyone share a moment like that?

Sometimes things keep us from putting God first, but God wants us to follow Him because we love Him. How can we show we love God? We can serve, worship, and obey God. Joshua left the people with an example of what it means to serve, worship, and obey God. After Jesus died on the cross and was raised from the dead, He gave the disciples instructions to make disciples of all nations, baptizing them in the name of the Father and of the Son and of the Holy Spirit, teaching them to obey everything Jesus commanded. (Matthew 28:19-20).

****

****

"Joshua 24:15
Joshua said ... "But as for me and my household, we will serve the Lord.""

****

****

"As Joshua prepared for his own death, he left behind a legacy of obedience to God. After Jesus' death and resurrection, He appeared to the disciples and left them with a legacy: to make disciples of all nations, baptizing them in the name of the Father and of the Son and of the Holy Spirit, teaching them to obey everything Jesus commanded. (Matthew 28:19-20)

As you share the story of Joshua's legacy with kids, point them to a greater legacy found in Jesus Christ. After Christ's resurrection, He sent His disciples out to tell the nations about Him. Jesus calls all people who trust in Him to tell others about Him- to serve Him."

Lets do it!

Materials required: A4 size white Canvas sheet, pencil, Acrylic paint colors

Ignite your cretaivity and with the help of your teacher and class team, each child will make the canvas painting for the memory verse as shown below:

Source: https://i.pinimg.com/564x/6c/d5/0a/6cd50a74e9ced5e323cdff102e2f6b0d.jpg

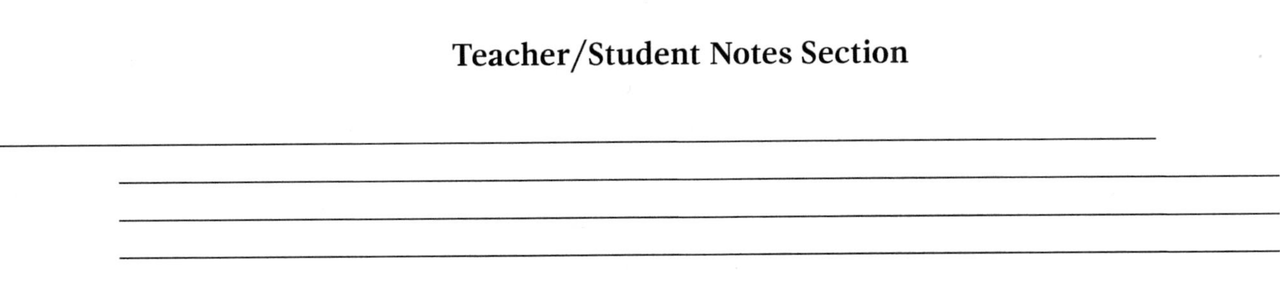

Teacher/Student Notes Section

Prayer

Ask one of the children in the group if she/he would like to lead the class in prayer (to pray for their classmates, family, church, teachers and pastors, and on what they learnt).

CHAPTER THIRTY

The Judges

Session Starter

Song:

God set judges over Israel
One brave woman, 11 men
They helped Israel fight their battles. Bring them back to God from sin
Othniel, Ehud, Shamgar, Deborah, Gideon, Tola, Jair, Jephthah,
Ibzan, Elon, Abdon, and Samson

Judges 1- 3, 10-12, 17-21

(Encourage children to open their bibles to the story portion. This lesson is an overview of the Judges of Israel. Teachers can summarize the portion from the Bible.)

Explain

After Joshua died, for a very long time his people kept their promise to God and they prospered and choose Judges to rule over them. However, when that generation passed away, the promises that were made to God were forgotten. Many of the Israelites forgot God. They began to worship idols of their neighbours and did wrong things that God did not like. God grew very angry. God would hand them to the hands of oppresor to punish them. Israel would then cry out to God and God would raise Judges to help Israel through Judge. And this cycle continued .. again and again:

- Israelites would abandon God and worship idols.
- God would send them an oppressor to punish his people.
- The Israelites would cry out to the LORD for help.
- God would raise a Judge to rescue his people.
- The Judge would drive out the oppressor and rescue God's people.
- The Israelites would worship and serve the LORD only.

The book of Judges lists twelve:

- Othniel (Judges 3:7–11)
- Ehud (Judges 3:12-22).
- Shamgar (Judges 3:31)
- Deborah (Judges 4-5)
- Gideon (Judges 6-8)
- Tola (Judges 10:1),
- Jair (Judges 10:3-5),
- Jephthah (Judges 10:6–12:7)
- Ibzan (Judges 12:8-11)
- Elon (Judges 12:11-12)
- Abdon (Judges 12:14-15)
- Samson (Judges 13-16)

There are also a few other important leaders in Judges, like Barak. However, they're not usually grouped with the twelve featured in the book of Judges.

The stories of some of the more well-known judges (like Deborah, Gideon and Samson) are covered in several chapters, while others only get a paragraph. Shamgar gets a single verse. In this lesson, we'll look at each of the judges, exploring the roles they played in delivering Israel. Some of the Judges will be covered in more details in the next few chapters.

Let's meet our judges.

Othniel

Othniel was the first judge, and he freed Israel from the oppression of King Cushan-Risathaim. His wife Achsah was given to him for conquering a city called Debir.

Ehud

Ehud was a skilled left-handed warrior, which allowed him to deceive King Eglon's guards and bring a sword into Eglon's royal chamber. Ehud said he had a "secret message" for Eglon and then drove the blade all the way into his stomach. In the ensuing confusion, his army drove out Eglon's forces.

Shamgar

Shamgar killed six hundred Philistines with an oxgoad, which is basically an ancient cattle prod. Did he kill them all at once, or over many battles? We don't know.

Deborah

Deborah is the only female judge, and she was also a prophetess. After freeing the Israelites from King Jabin, she wrote The Song of Deborah (Judges 5) which is believed to be one of the oldest passages of the Bible.

Gideon

Gideon is one of the most well-known and important leaders from the Book of Judges. There are more verses dedicated to him than any other judge. Gideon had a miraculous birth, and when he grew up he was called to free the Israelites from Midian. He defeated their armies with just 300 men. The Israelites tried to make him their king, but he refused.

Tola

Tola became judge after the death of Abimilech, an evil son of Gideon who had led many Israelites astray. He was from the tribe of Issachar, and his grandfather was a man named Dodo. He led Israel for 23 years. The Bible says he "rose to save Israel" (Judges 10:1), but we don't know what from.

Jair

Jair led Israel for 22 years. His claim to fame is that he had 30 sons who rode 30 donkeys and ruled 30 towns, which were called the "towns of Jair."

Jephthah

Jephthah was a mighty warrior who made a foolish vow, saved the Israelites, and then did something terrible: he sacrificed his own daughter because of his vow.

Ibzan

Ibzan had 30 sons and 30 daughters, all of whom married people outside his tribe—possibly to extend his family's influence. He judged Israel for seven years.

Elon

Elon is the most unknown judge. About all we can gather is that he was from the tribe of Zebulun, and his name means a type of tree—either an "oak" or "terebinth" (we're not sure which one).

Abdon

Abdon was probably a very wealthy judge, because about all we know about him is that he had forty sons and thirty grandsons who rode on seventy donkeys. He led Israel for eight years.

Samson

Samson is the strongest person in the Bible, and his life's purpose was pretty much to wreak havoc on the Philistines. Samson was a Nazarite, and from the time he was born, he never cut his hair. This was the key to his strength *and* his Achilles' heel. He was eventually captured after his lover tricked him into revealing his secret. When his hair grew back, he ripped out the pillars of a building, killing himself and 3,000 Philistines.

Source: https://overviewbible.com/wp-content/uploads/2020/03/Judges.jpg

The final section of the Book of Judges, chapters(17-21), contains very disturbing stories of idolatory and injustice. Each story begins and concludes with an identical opening "In those days there was no king in Israel; all the people did what was right in their own eyes".

It becomes clear from these stories that the moral corruption within Israel is going to be solved by one thing alone: Israel needed a good king!

Each time the Israelites went around the cycle, their spiritual condition got worse and worse. Israel needed a good King. Jesus came and gave us the perfect example. He died and was resurrected on the third day and is seated as the King of Kings, Lord of Lords!

Judges show the need for godly leadership. God appoints godly leaders for us, like Pastors, Leaders, Parents, and Bible Teachers, to guide us in Godly ways. Honoring and submitting to Godly leadership is important.

Discuss:

- Share with your class any experience you may have when you may have felt spiritually weak and were strengthened by your elders or friends.
- Explain and ask for feedback on the following " How important is fellowship with God AND fellowship with brethren.

****

Memory Verse

****

"Judges 3:15
Again the Israelites cried out to the Lord, and he gave them a deliverer.."

****

Christ Connect

****

"God sent his only son Jesus because He loves us. He did not forsake us but sent his only son to forgive us our sins and bring us close to Him. Turn to God and repent of your sins and He will deliver you."

Write the days' verse on paper and draw a big heart around it and colour it. Draw a line from the heart to make it look like a string. Now you have a heart shaped balloon. You can write Jesus loves you along the string line (a model is shown below).

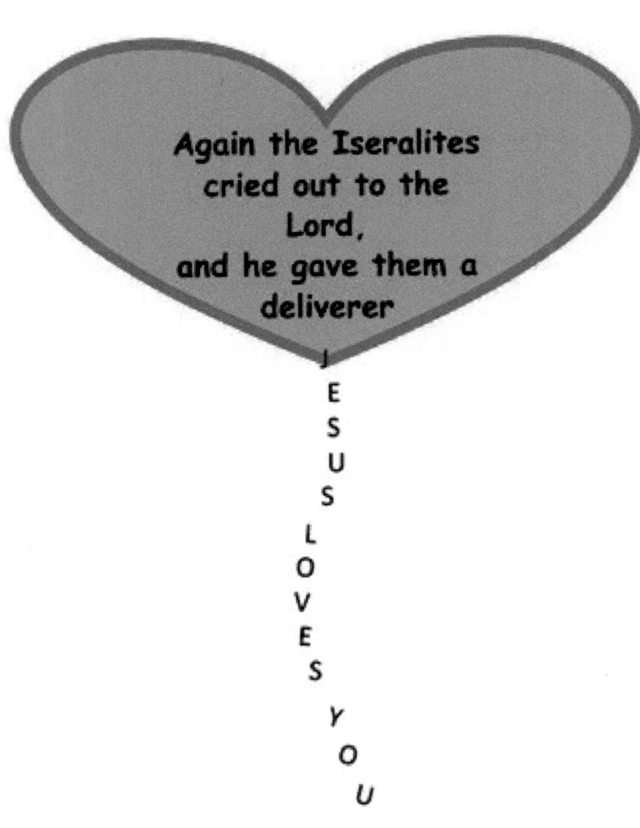

Teacher/Student Notes Section

Prayer

Ask one of the children in the group if she/he would like to lead the class in prayer (to pray for their classmates, family, church, teachers and pastors, and on what they learnt).

CHAPTER THIRTY-ONE

DEBORAH AND BARAK

Session Starter

The Good and the Bad

Ask kids to sort the items according to what they think is healthy and what they think is unhealthy. Discuss the choices. Ask kids to sort the items again by what they think is good to eat (they like it) and what they think is bad to eat (they don't like to eat it). Is what we think is good to eat always healthy to eat? Are some of the things that are good to eat (tasty) unhealthy for us? Do we always know what is good for us in life? Sometimes God knows something is good for us, but we aren't sure it is good. God always does what is good for His people. Listen to today's Bible story to discover the good God wants for His people.

Judges 4-5

(Encourage children to open their bibles to the story portion)

After the judges Ehud and Shamgar died, the Israelites forgot about God. So, God allowed the king of Canaan to overtake Israel under the leadership of a cruel army commander Sisera for 20 years. Israel remembered God and they cried out to God, to save them.

Deborah was the judge of Israel at this time. One day, Deborah called for Barak and said, "God wants you to gather 10,000 men. Lead them to Mount Tabor. God will help you defeat Sisera there." Barak said to Deborah, "I will go if you will come with me. If you won't come, I'm not going." "I'll go," Deborah said. "But you will receive no honour for the battle."

So, Deborah, Barak, and 10,000 men went to Mount Tabor. Sisera heard that Barak was at Mount Tabor, and he took his 900 chariots and all his men to fight. "Barak, go! God will help you defeat Sisera today," Deborah said. Barak and his 10,000 men moved down the mountain toward Sisera and his army.

The LORD confused Sisera and all of the army. Barak chased the chariots and the army, and everyone in the army was killed by the sword. None of them survived, but Sisera had escaped! Sisera went to the tent of Jael because he and Jael's husband were friends. Jael said, "Come in. Don't be afraid." Jael gave Sisera something to drink and covered him with a rug. Sisera was so exhausted that he fell into a deep sleep. Jael knew that Sisera was an evil man, an enemy of God.

She took a tent peg and a hammer, and she drove the tent peg through Sisera's head, killing him while he slept. Barak arrived, looking for Sisera. Jael greeted him and said, "I will show you the man you are looking for." Barak went into her tent and saw Sisera lying dead with a tent peg through his head. That day, God allowed the Israelites to defeat the king of Canaan. The Israelites had won the battle! Deborah and Barak sang a victory song. They praised God for helping them beat the Canaanites. The land was peaceful for 40 more years.

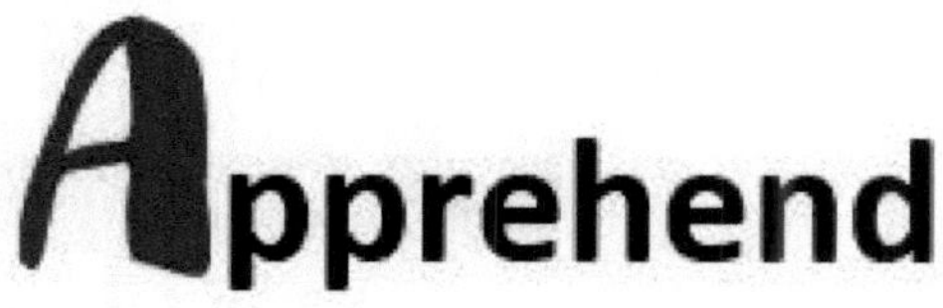

The Israelites lived for 20 years under a cruel ruler as a consequence of their sin. They remembered the peace they had when they loved and followed God, and they cried out to God to rescue them again. God sent Deborah, a judge and prophetess, to deliver the people. Deborah called for Barak to lead God's people to fight the Canaanites.

The Israelites defeated the Canaanites and lived in peace for 40 years. Did you notice how the Israelites won the battle? God fought for them again. God confused the enemy's army and Israel won the battle.

What is the goal of God's plan? (God's plan is to bring about His glory and our good.)

****

Memory Verse

****

“Judges 5:3
“Hear, O kings; give ear, O princes; to the Lord I will sing;
I will make melody to the Lord, the God of Israel.”

****

Christ Connect

****

- ***God does what is for His glory and our good. (Psalm 115:3; Romans 8:28). God fought for the Israelites and used Deborah, Barak, and Jael to defeat Canaan. In a similar way, God uses people and events to not only save us from our enemies, but to bring about our ultimate good.***

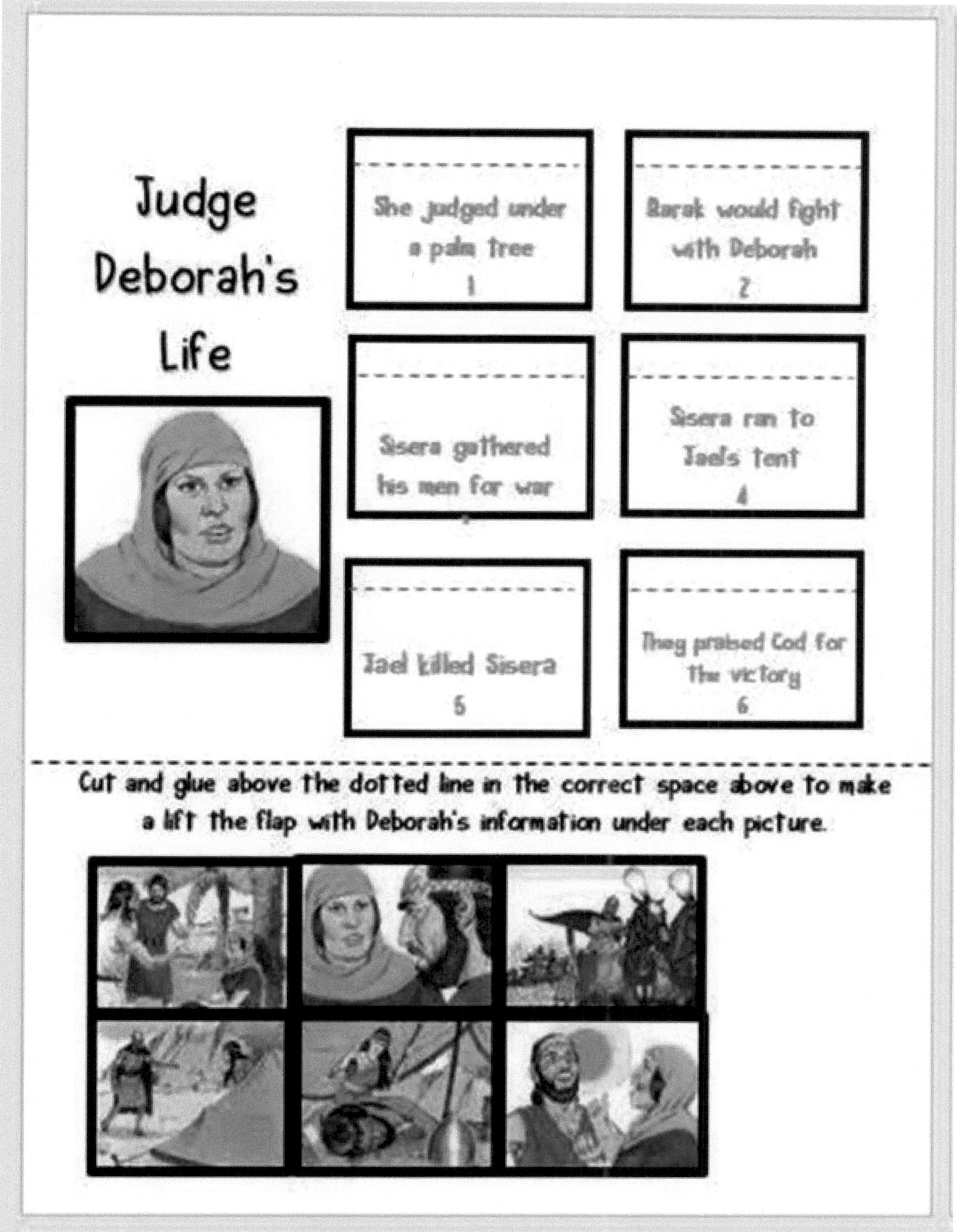

Source: https://4.bp.blogspot.com

Teacher/Student Notes Section

____

____

____

____

Prayer

Ask one of the children in the group if she/he would like to lead the class in prayer (to pray for their classmates, family, church, teachers and pastors, and on what they learnt).

CHAPTER THIRTY-TWO

GIDEON

Session Starter

What's so Hard About That?

Ask the kids to think about things that are difficult for them to do, and create a list on the paper.

Ask what kind of help they would need to accomplish the tasks listed.

Explain that Gideon thought it was impossible for God to give them victory over their enemies. He tested God two times to prove that He would keep His promise to help His people. We can trust God to help us when we step out in faith.

Judges 6-8
(Encourage children to open their bibles to the story portion)

Once again, the people of Israel did what was evil in the sight of the Lord. So, for seven years he handed them over to the people of Midian. The Midianites treated the people of Israel very badly. That's why they made hiding places for themselves. They hid in holes in the mountains. They also hid in caves and other safe places.

The angel of the Lord appeared to Gideon. He said, "Mighty warrior, the Lord is with you." "But sir," Gideon replied, "you say the Lord is with us. Then why has all of this happened to us? Where are all of the wonderful things he has done? Our parents told us about them. They said, 'Didn't the Lord bring us up out of Egypt?' But now the Lord has deserted us. He has handed us over to Midian."

The Lord turned to Gideon. He said to him, "You are strong. Go and save Israel from the power of Midian. I am sending you." "But Lord," Gideon asked, "how can I possibly save Israel? My family group is the weakest in the tribe of Manasseh. And I'm the least important member of my family." The Lord answered, "I will be with you. So, you will strike down the men of Midian all at one time."

The Lord spoke to Gideon. He said, "I want to hand Midian over to you. But you have too many men for me to do that. I do not want Israel to brag that their own strength has saved them. So here is what I want you to announce to your men. Tell them, 'Those who tremble with fear can turn back. They can leave Mount Gilead." So, 22,000 men left. But 10,000 remained. The Lord spoke to Gideon again. He said, "There are still too many men. So, take them down to the water. I will sort them out for you there. If I say, 'This one will go with you,' he will go. But if I say, 'That one will not go with you,' he will not go."

So, Gideon took the men down to the water. There the Lord spoke to him. He said, "Some men will drink the way dogs do. They will lap up the water with their tongues. Separate them from those who get down on their knees to drink."

Three hundred men lapped up the water. They brought it up to their mouths with their hands. All of the rest got down on their knees to drink. The Lord spoke to Gideon. He said, "With the help of the 300 men who lapped up the water I will save you. I will hand the Midianites over to you. Let all of the other men go home." So, Gideon sent the rest of the men of Israel to their tents. But he kept the 300 men. They took over the supplies and trumpets the others had left. The Midianites had set up their camp in the valley below where Gideon was.

Then Gideon worshiped God. He returned to the camp of Israel. He called out, "Get up! The Lord has handed the Midianites over to you." Gideon separated the 300 men into three companies. He put a trumpet and an empty jar into the hands of each man. And he put a torch inside each jar. "Watch me," he told them. "Do what I do. I'll go to the edge of the enemy camp. Then do exactly as I do. I and everyone who is with me will blow our trumpets. Then blow your trumpets from your positions all around the camp. And shout the battle cry, 'For the Lord and for Gideon!" Gideon and the 100 men who were with him reached the edge of the enemy camp. It was about ten o'clock at night. It was just after the guard had been changed. Gideon and his men blew their trumpets. They broke the jars that were in their hands. The three companies blew their trumpets. They smashed their jars. They held their torches in their left hands. They held in their right hands the trumpets they were going to blow. Then they shouted the battle cry, "A sword for the Lord and for Gideon!"

Each man stayed in his position around the camp. But all of the Midianites ran away in fear. They were crying out as they ran. When the 300 trumpets were blown, the Lord caused all of the men in the enemy camp to start fighting each other. They attacked each other with their swords.

Review

God Has a Plan Even When Life is Hard. Though Gideon's people had turned their back on God and were reaping the consequences, the Lord still heard their cries of distress. No matter how ugly our circumstances get, no matter how far we have wandered, God is still faithful, and He still has a plan for our good and our future.

Confronting Our Idols and Insecurity. God calls us to worship Him alone, with uncompromising devotion. Before Gideon could lead his people to bravely face their oppressors, he first had to confront his people's idolatry and his own insecurities.

Our Doubts and Fears Don't Disqualify Us from God's Plan. Through Gideon's story, we see that God is much bigger than our weaknesses, and He takes great and gracious measures to overcome our trepidation and our fears, so that we can serve Him with a brave heart.

The Dark Side of Success and Power. The Bible doesn't sugar-coat people's weaknesses; it gives us the good, the bad, and the ugly, so that we might learn to "guard your heart above all else, for it determines the course of your life."

****

Memory Verse

****

"Judges 6:8-10
8 he sent them a prophet, who said, "This is what the Lord, the God of Israel, says: I brought you up out of Egypt, out of the land of slavery. 9 I rescued you from the hand of the Egyptians. .....But you have not listened to me.""

****

Christ Connect

****

"The rescue God accomplishes through Gideon demonstrates the power of the LORD to use a humble warrior to overcome a strong enemy. This is a pattern for the coming Kingdom of Christ, when Jesus overcomes all nations through the witness of the church.
God saved the Israelites with only 300 men to show His power and to make sure that the Israelites knew that salvation was through God alone. God wanted to make sure that no one could boast in their own strength or think that they had fought the battle on their own. The same is true for us when we think about salvation."

Do

T	T	R	R	N	W	O	N	G	M	X	Q	V	K	S
O	O	K	O	W	B	M	W	D	U	L	C	V	M	C
O	R	D	J	B	V	I	I	O	O	R	R	T	P	T
M	C	F	L	D	W	D	O	T	X	D	H	L	E	P
A	H	H	G	E	A	I	V	C	L	A	N	C	I	M
N	E	L	I	R	T	A	S	U	M	E	N	M	P	S
Y	S	D	D	D	E	N	T	V	G	L	A	S	L	D
H	K	I	E	N	R	I	E	D	Q	I	V	R	E	Q
L	K	P	O	U	B	T	P	R	O	G	G	E	S	H
A	X	M	N	H	H	E	M	I	T	T	R	H	P	I
P	D	W	L	E	C	S	U	N	H	N	P	C	K	E
P	O	L	A	E	O	J	R	K	K	U	Z	T	S	N
E	F	G	G	R	Y	S	T	N	W	O	L	I	N	P
D	P	S	H	H	K	Z	M	V	W	M	P	P	U	T
X	Q	Z	G	T	E	K	N	E	E	S	I	G	W	L

DRINK
GIDEON
ISRAEL
KNEES
LAPPED

MIDIANITES
MOUNT GILEAD
PITCHERS
THREE HUNDRED

TOO MANY
TORCHES
TRUMPETS
WATER

Source: https://biblepathwayadventures.com

Teacher/Student Notes Section

____
____
____
____

Prayer

Ask one of the children in the group if she/he would like to lead the class in prayer (to pray for their classmates, family, church, teachers and pastors, and on what they learnt).

CHAPTER THIRTY-THREE

Samson

Session Starter

Invite the kids to compete against each other with common exercises. Consider forming two groups—boys and girls. Try some of the following ideas:

Who can do the most jumping jacks in one minute?
Who can do the most push-ups?
Who can stand on one leg the longest?
Who can do the most sit-ups in one minute?
Who can stand on their tiptoes the longest?

Physical exercise makes our bodies stronger, but it won't make us perfect. Samson was very strong, but he still struggled with sin. What should we do when we sin? We should ask God for forgiveness.

Judges 13-16
(Encourage children to open their bibles to the story portion)

The Israelites disobeyed God, so God handed them over to their enemies, the Philistines, for 40 years. But not all of the Israelites disobeyed God. Some of them still worshiped Him. Two of those people were Manoah and his wife. One day the Angel of the LORD appeared to Manoah's wife and told her she would have a son. Her son would belong to God. God had special instructions for the baby's life: he should never cut his hair. God said, "Your son will be a Nazirite. He is going to save the Israelites from the Philistines."

Manoah's wife had a baby, and she named him Samson. As Samson grew, God blessed him. God gave Samson great strength. When Samson grew up, he saw a Philistine woman he wanted to marry. He went to her town to talk to her. As he traveled with his father and mother, a young lion jumped out at him. Samson killed the lion with his bare hands. Samson did not tell his parents what he had done. After some time, Samson traveled again to marry the woman. Samson found the lion's carcass. A swarm of bees had made honey in the carcass. Samson scooped some honey into his hands and gave some to his parents.

The Philistines sent 30 men to help Samson prepare the wedding feast. He told the men a riddle: Out of the eater came something to eat, and out of the strong came something sweet. Samson was talking about the lion and the honey, but none of the men could solve the riddle. They asked Samson's new wife to help them. Samson's wife cried until Samson told her the answer to the riddle. Then Samson's wife told the men the answer. Samson had been tricked! He was angry, and he left his wife.

Later on, Samson went back to get his wife. But her father had given her to another man. "I thought you hated her," he said. Samson was so mad that he went out and caught 300 foxes. He tied their tails together with a torch and sent them out into the Philistines' fields. The foxes burned up the fields. The Philistines went to find Samson to punish him. The men of Judah had tied him up with ropes, but Samson was so strong that he broke through the ropes. He took the jawbone of a donkey and killed 1,000 men with it. Samson escaped to the capital city of Gaza. The Philistines found him there and planned to kill him. Samson fell in love with a woman named Delilah. The Philistines talked to Delilah. "Get Samson to tell you why he is so strong," they said. "We will each give you 1,100 pieces of silver." Delilah asked Samson why he was so strong. She tested him with seven fresh bowstrings and with new ropes. She tried weaving the braids on his head, but nothing took away Samson's strength. Delilah begged Samson to tell her the truth, so Samson did. "If you cut my hair, I will not have my strength." Delilah sent for the Philistine leaders. They waited until Samson was sleeping, then a man cut his hair. Delilah woke him up. "Samson! Wake up! The Philistines are here to kill you!" But Samson's strength had left him. The Philistines seized him and made him blind. They took him away in shackles and made fun of him.

Samson's hair began to grow back. One day, the Philistines made Samson stand between two pillars in the temple of Dagon, the Philistines' god. Samson cried out to God, "Lord GOD, please remember me. Strengthen me once more." So God strengthened Samson. Samson pushed on the pillars and collapsed the temple. Samson and all of the Philistines in it died.

- What did the Angel of the LORD tell Samson's mother not to cut? (Samson's hair)
- What did Samson use to kill 1,000 Philistines? (a jawbone from a donkey)
- Who told the Philistines that Samson's strength was tied to his hair? (Delilah)
- How was Samson able to push down the posts holding up the false god's temple? (He asked God to give him strength one more time)
- What should I do when I sin? (I should ask God for forgiveness.)

****

Memory Verse

****

"Judges 13: 24
The woman gave birth to a boy and named him Samson. He grew and the Lord blessed him."

****

Christ Connect

****

"God raised up Samson as the last judge to deliver the Israelites from thePhilistines. Samson killed more Philistines in his death than he did in his life. Jesus came as the last Deliverer, all those who accept Christ as their savior is saved."

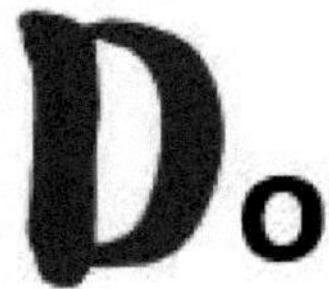

Samson did not protect his Spiritual strength.

Source: : https://coloringhome.com/coloring/qcB/9oo/qcB9oo4c5.jpg

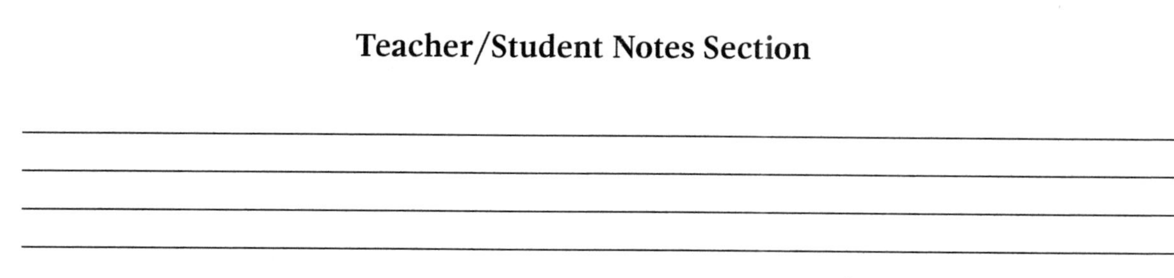

Teacher/Student Notes Section

Prayer

Ask one of the children in the group if she/he would like to lead the class in prayer (to pray for their classmates, family, church, teachers and pastors, and on what they learnt).

CHAPTER THIRTY-FOUR

RUTH AND BOAZ

Session Starter

Teacher will hand each child with a fruit card. Every child will hold up their card and tell if it is a fruit they like. If the fruit card is not the fruit they like, the teacher can provide an alternate one (fruit of their choice). Say: God gives us food to eat. Today we will see how God used Boaz to provide food to Ruth.

Ruth 1-4
(Encourage children to open their bibles to the story portion)

Explain

Today, we will hear a beautiful story of a woman named Ruth. The story of Ruth begins in the journey of the family of Elimelech and his wife, Naomi, along with their two sons, who left Bethelem (their hometown) because of famine, to the land of Moab for food. The two sons grew and took Moabite wives, something that by tradition in the Jewish faith was not encouraged. Marrying a Canaanite and those living within the borders of the promised land) was against the law set (Deuteronomy 7:1-4). But in this story, we see how Ruth, a Moabite woman, was used by God.

The famine had ended in Judah, so Naomi decided to return. Naomi encouraged Orpah (the widow of her first son) and Ruth (the widow of her second son) to return to their families. The women were very sad to leave each other. However, Orpah returned back to her home, but Ruth clung to Naomi. Ruth said, "Wherever you go, I will go, and wherever you live, I will live; your people will be my people, and your God will be my God," Ruth said. So Naomi returned to Bethlehem with her daughter-in-law (Ruth) at the beginning of the barley harvest.

Naomi asked Ruth permission to go into the fields and gather fallen grain. She happened to go to the field of Boaz, a good man from the family of Naomi's late husband, Elimelech. Boaz saw Ruth in his field. He had heard how kind Ruth was to Naomi, staying with her after her husband died and leaving Moab to travel back to Bethlehem with her. Boaz told Ruth to stay in his field, where she would be safe. Boaz made sure Ruth had enough food. Ruth gathered plenty of grain in the field. She returned to Naomi and told her about Boaz. "Boaz is one of our family redeemers," Naomi replied.

A family redeemer was someone who would help his close relatives if they were in trouble. Naomi knew Boaz would take care of Ruth, so she encouraged Ruth to stay in his fields. Naomi wanted to make sure Ruth had a husband to care for her, so she gave Ruth special instructions. Ruth put on her best clothes and laid down near Boaz's feet. In this way, Ruth showed Boaz that she hoped he would marry her.

Boaz was surprised to find Ruth at his feet. "You are a family redeemer," she said. Boaz promised to redeem Ruth, which meant he would buy back the land that Naomi sold after her husband died, and he would marry Ruth. He gave Ruth grain and sent her back to Naomi. Boaz bought back the land that had belonged to Naomi's husband and sons, and he married Ruth. Ruth and Boaz had a son named Obed. Naomi took care of Obed. When Obed grew up, he was the father of Jesse, who was the father of King David.

Review Questions:

- Who did Ruth want to marry? (Boaz)
- How did Boaz know that Ruth wanted to marry him? (She lay down at his feet during the night.)
- How did Naomi's relative show that he gave Boaz permission to marry Ruth? (He passed on his sandal.)

- What was the name of Ruth and Boaz' son? (Obed)

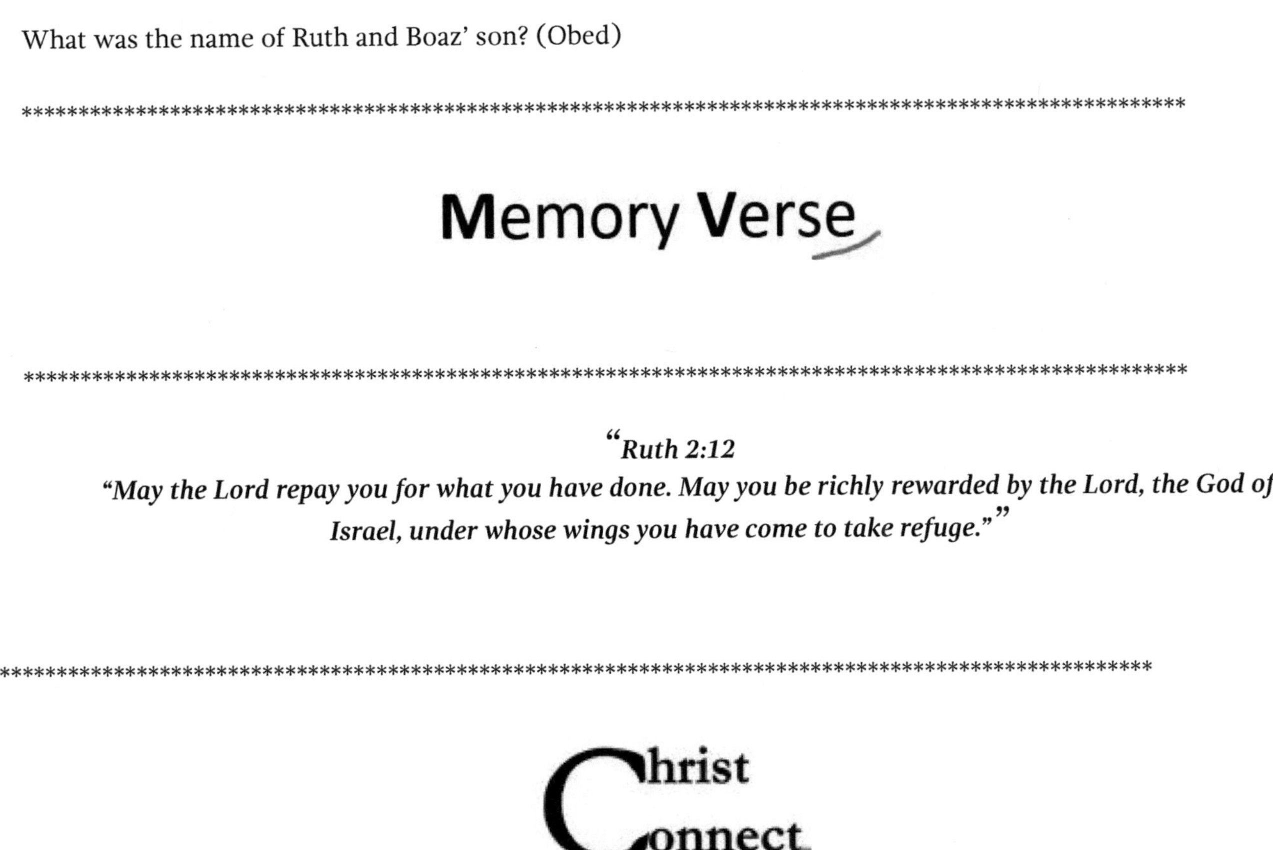

****

Memory Verse

****

"Ruth 2:12
"May the Lord repay you for what you have done. May you be richly rewarded by the Lord, the God of Israel, under whose wings you have come to take refuge.""

****

Christ Connect

****

"Jesus, similar to Boaz, is our redeemer. We are like the widowed foreigner with no good in us, but God loved us just the same and sought to redeem us to give us a hope and a future. But God being a just God, He sent His son Jesus for us, to justly pay with His life to redeem us. Through Jesus alone we get the prvildege of being restored back in to the family of God. When we accept Jesus as our savior we are heirs of God and co-heirs with Christ.
We respond to such redeeming love- by remaining loyal and faithful. "

Do

Questions	Answers
____ Where was Ruth born?	1. Feast of Shavuot (Pentecost)
____ What was the name of Ruth's sister-in-law?	2. Boaz's field
____ With whom did Ruth move to Bethlehem?	3. Six measures of barley
____ Where did Ruth and Boaz first meet?	4. Land of Moab
____ What did Boaz offer Ruth to eat?	5. At Boaz's feet
____ On the threshing floor, where did Ruth sleep?	6. Judah
____ The next morning, what did Boaz give Ruth?	7. Naomi
____ Boaz was of which tribe of Israel? (1 Chronicles 2)	8. Obed
____ Which of God's Appointed Times (Feasts) celebrates the wheat harvest?	9. Orpah
____ After Ruth and Boaz were married, what did they name their son?	10. Bread and roasted grain

Source: https://biblepathwayadventures.com/wp-content/uploads/2017/05/Ruth-Boaz1.png

Teacher/Student Notes Section

____
____
____
____

Prayer

Ask one of the children in the group if she/he would like to lead the class in prayer (to pray for their classmates, family, church, teachers and pastors, and on what they learnt).

Source Of Title Pictures

Lesson 1: https://m.media-amazon.com/images/I/71bWFDWldKL._AC_SX466_.jpg

Lesson 2: https://www.kingjamesbibleonline.org/Inspirational-Images/large/Genesis_1-1.jpg

Lesson 3:
https://assetsnffrgfa.akamaihd.net/assets/m/1102012650/univ/art/1102012650_univ_cnt_1_xl.jpg

Lesson 4: https://communication.cph.org/hubfs/_blogs/CPH_blog/Teach/2021/03/adam-eve.jpg

Lesson 5: https://media.freebibleimages.org/stories/FB_Cain_Abel/overview-images/002-cain-abel.jpg?1635949554

Lesson 6: https://wp.biologos.org/wp-content/uploads/2019/01/noahs-ark-genesis.jpg

Lesson 7: https://www.gaia.com/wp-content/uploads/article-migration-image-Tower-of-Babel-Bible.jpg

Lesson 8: http://wordexplain.com/images/Abraham_descendants_as_stars-802x883.jpg

Lesson 9: https://medium.com/bible-and-prayer-book/abraham-isaac-sacrifice-c435bd5f0453

Lesson 10: https://www.biblestudytools.com/bible-stories/jacob-s-ladder-bible-story.html

Lesson 11: https://st-takla.org/Gallery/var/albums/Bible/Illustrations/Bible-Slides/OT/01-Genesis/www-St-Takla-org--Bible-Slides-genesis-140.jpg

Lesson 12: https://images.subsplash.com/image.jpg?id=503194bf-7d6f-4ca7-927b-7b672654c438&w=1280&h=720

Lesson 13: https://media.freebibleimages.org/stories/FB_YO_Joseph_Dreams/overview-images/002-yo-joseph-dreams.jpg?1613597970

Lesson 14: https://sundayschoolzone.com/wp-content/uploads/2018/12/OT05L4_1000-283x283.jpg

Lesson 15: https://exodusfromegypt.com/2016/11/23/exodus-from-egypt-the-first-and-second-exodus-2ed/

Lesson 16: https://www.thejc.com/judaism/features/why-did-we-sing-when-the-egyptians-drowned-1.54039

Lesson 17: https://www.rainbowtoken.com/exodus-16-manna-and-quail-from-heaven.html

Lesson 18: https://www.gospelimages.com/images/content/paintings/84/image_the_golden_calf_-gospel_images_normal.jpg

Lesson 19: https://www.bibleiq.org/wp-content/uploads/2020/04/Two-Greastest-Commandments-graphic.png

Lesson 20: https://i.pinimg.com/564x/3c/7b/4c/3c7b4c61a54b05ca328c14324a0fa1d0.jpg

Lesson 21: https://www.messianic-revolution.com/wp-content/uploads/2016/05/Framework-and-Tabernacle-Layers-Lesson-23.jpg

Lesson 22: https://in.pinterest.com/pin/317503842461717016/

Lesson 23: https://www.shutterstock.com/image-vector/vector-illustration-christian-worship-hands-raising-253498822

Lesson 24: https://s3.amazonaws.com/focus.cinevee.com/ttwmk-live/item/912/AdobeStock_4053703.jpg

Lesson 25: https://i.pinimg.com/564x/5d/47/cc/5d47ccc49b7763d61f04a58208f24515.jpg

Lesson 26: http s://i.pinimg.com/564x/79/96/de/7996ded6391ca4866dd97571e44ef900.jpg

Lesson 27: http://storage.snappages.site/CPHJQN/assets/images/2691770_500x375_2500.jpg

Lesson 28: https://i.pinimg.com/564x/9b/e4/e5/9be4e517ea788cba7c5b1b741e65dec1.jpg

Lesson 29: https://cbcjamaica.files.wordpress.com/2013/12/joshua-remember-the-people.jpg

Lesson 30: https://i0.wp.com/jeremymavis.com/wp-content/uploads/2016/02/List-of-Judges.jpg?fit=1024%2C576&ssl=1

Lesson 31: https://www.fbceastman.com/download_file/view_inline/1405/

Lesson 32: https://i0.wp.com/ministry-to-children.com/wp-content/uploads/2019/11/gideons-army-1.jpg?w=360&ssl=1

Lesson 33: https://quizizz.com/media/resource/gs/quizizz-media/quizzes/69d298b9-8d13-46f0-9182-c8f75e3ca683

Lesson 34: https://i.pinimg.com/564x/ec/7b/62/ec7b62efd20fe1738e5c1b9de399bde5.jpg

Epilogue

"How can a young person stay on the path of purity? By living according to your word". (Psalms 119:9)
"Train up a child in the way he should go; even when he is old he will not depart from it." (Proverbs 22:6)

Children are a gift from God and it is important to bring them up in the ways of God. At Master's Grace Church, we believe that it is very important to mentor a child and help them thrive on the Word of God. This is only possible by providing them with the right teaching and learning environment. We sensed a need for concise teaching resources with practical anecdotes and examples, and that is how the idea of this book My Bible Study Book was conceived.

This book is the first of a three-volume curriculum, developed to teach the Bible and train children at the kindergarten level. This book is a collective effort of the members of Sapphires, the Women's Ministry team at Master's Grace Church.

We consulted mothers, fathers, Bible teachers, Pastors, and youngsters at various stages of the production. The book that you are holding is the is a result of the combined efforts of all these men and women. To keep it simple, precise and concise, this book was subject to several stages of rework, revision and continuous feedback from multiple sources.

We sincerely hope and pray My Bible Study Book will be a blessed resource for Sunday school teachers, leaders and children of all age groups. We sincerely pray that this book will be a very helpful tool in the journey of children in learning Bible; the Word of God.

Blessings,

Pastors Joseph Thomas & Mini Thomas

About The Authors

Pr. Mini Thomas is one of the founding members of Mater's Grace Church (MGC). She is a teacher at heart and by profession. She is the driving force behind making this vision a reality. She co-pastors MGC with her husband Pr. Joseph Thomas and are parents of two handsome adult twins. Besides her full-time job as a professor with a Master of Engineering and a research scholar, she has a Master's in Divinity and heads the Children's Ministry at MGC. Pr. Mini and her family reside in Mississauga, Ontario.

Berlin Chandra serves as the leader of the Children's Ministry at MGC. She attributes her passion for developing children to the Sunday School and Vacation Bible Schools she had attended as a child. Berlin has been instrumental in organizing events for children in the church. She and her husband have two lovely girls and live in Milton, Ontario. She possesses an MBA and works a full-time job.

Nissy Varghese serves at MGC in more than one capacity. As a talented artist, she is our 'go-to' person for anything in the creative space. She is passionate about using her talents to benefit little children and adults alike. She and her husband are parents of a handsome little champ and live in Toronto, Ontario. Besides, she has a Masters in Community Health Nursing and enjoys teaching, doodling, painting, and gardening.

Monisha Steeve also has been one of the teachers at MGC since we started. Besides teaching the children, she also plays a key role in the hospitality and the welcome team of the church. She enjoys cooking and is a respiratory therapist. She and her husband are parents of two blessed children; a daughter and a son. They live in Mississauga, Ontario.

Printed by Libri Plureos GmbH in Hamburg,
Germany